Praise

Unintended Conseque

"Everyone has had their Invincible moment ... that instant when all of the odds and adversity are conquered and your goal has been achieved or your 'dream' has been realized. Bill Shaner had everything but his life and family taken away from him but somehow he showed us true courage by never quitting. He nearly paid the ultimate price but was willing to pay the price to make his dream to be whole once again come true. A great story about faith, guts and Invincibility!"

~ Vince Papale, former Philadelphia Eagles football player, author of the book *Invincible: My Journey from Fan to NFL Team Captain* whose character was played by Mark Wahlberg in the Disney movie *Invincible*.

"Bill Shaner's life illustrates that an unfortunate experience can leave you not only wiser, but more honest with yourself, compassionate, giving, caring and most important willing and able to create your best life."

~ Maureen Whitehouse, expert in personal development and enlightenment and the best-selling author of *Soul-Full Eating* (www. soul-fulleating.com)

"Bill Shaner has showered the reader with his potent choices to embrace a life which SHINES with the possible. You will find his impressive book to be an invitation to that choice to shine."

~ Bob Danzig, former CEO of Hearst Newspapers; Author; Hall of Fame Speaker

"Bill Shaner's remarkable story will leave you resonating with inspiration. But perhaps most importantly, he goes beyond his near-death experience and gives us a game plan for living life to the fullest. He has left a blueprint on how to be positive and patient, on how to connect with people and find inner peace. With apologies to Neil Armstrong, Shaner's story can be summed up thusly: One small collapsed building on a man, one giant step for mankind."

~ Sam Carchidi, author of *Miracle in the Making: The Adam Taliaferro Story* and *Standing Tall: The Kevin Everett Story*

"Shaner effectively relates the highly dramatic story of his accident and the lessons learned thereafter in a concise, straightforward style that clearly displays his spirit, personality and humor. Part memoir, part blueprint for life change, *Unintended Consequences* has a remarkable amount to offer readers."

~ Pamela Victor, *Feathered Quill Book Reviews*

"Filled with depth and wisdom, yet easy to read, *Unintended Consequences* explains how the Universe works and lovingly supports us."

~ Terri Amos-Britt, author of *The Enlightened Mom* and *Message Sent,* and founder of www.EnlightenedFamilyInstitute.com

"*Unintended Consequences* is a powerful inspirational book. It is well written, easy to read, and compelling. I highly recommend it."

~ Dean Portinga, author of *Spiritual Insights: A Whole New Understanding of the Ten Commandments*

"Unintended Consequences is the kind of book that makes you say, 'WOW!' If you are seeking a breakthrough, then this book is for you. There is something for you on every page. Read slowly. You are about to be transformed."

~ Lorna Owens, author of *Everyday Grace, Everyday Miracle: Living the Life You Were Born to Live* and host of *And the Women Gather* TV show

"The book will cause you to reflect on your own life and hopefully make a few changes to live your life for the better. Shaner is definitely a remarkable man who has been through a lot and I commend him for taking what could have been a devastatingly negative experience and turning it into one of growth and enlightenment."

~ Kam Aures, *Rebecca's Reads*

"Unintended Consequences illustrates the importance of faith, trust and sheer stubbornness. Extremely inspirational."

~ Tami Brady, *TCM Reviews*

"Bill Shaner will show you how you can – and how you do – create your reality. He's come back from what could be one of life's toughest challenges and he'll show you the tools he used."

~ W. Mitchell, author of *It's Not What Happens to You, It's What You Do About It*

"A great book filled with life-changing advice."

~ Maureen Stearns, author of *Conscious Courage: Turning Everyday Challenges into Opportunities*

"Bill Shaner has written a very inspiring book. His story will impact thousands of people. Get ready for an amazing reading experience."

~ Pat Williams, Sr. Vice President, Orlando Magic and author of *Extreme Dreams Depend on Teams*

"Shaner almost lost his life in a construction accident. He defeated the odds by walking again. The author's story includes his own insights and personal experiences of a transformation through tragedy."

~ Margaret Orford, *Allbooks Reviews*

"*Unintended Consequences* is a spiritual memoir from Bill Shaner as he reflects on his near-death experience and how his long journey back to life taught himself much about how the universe works. Imparting his wisdom, his advice is sound, making *Unintended Consequences* a unique and thought provoking read."

~ John Burroughs, *The Midwest Book Review*

UNINTENDED CONSEQUENCES

LESSONS FROM A LIFE ALMOST LOST

UNINTENDED CONSEQUENCES

LESSONS FROM A LIFE ALMOST LOST

BILL SHANER

PANTHA PUBLISHING
NAPLES, FLORIDA

UNINTENDED CONSEQUENCES
LESSONS FROM A LIFE ALMOST LOST

by Bill Shaner

Pantha Publishing
728 Carica Road, Naples, FL 34108
www.panthapublishing.com

A Note to Readers
This book tells my true story; all events are presented in actual chronology. All information including places and dates are accurate to the best knowledge of the author. Some names, however, have been changed to protect individuals' privacy.

Book cover design and book layout by James Arneson,
www.JaadBookDesign.com
Editorial services by Robin Quinn, Quinn's Word for Word,
www.writingandediting.biz

Publisher's Cataloging-in-Publication Data
Shaner, Bill
Unintended Consequences: Lessons From A Life Almost Lost / Bill Shaner
   p. cm.
   LCCN 2009900117
   ISBN-13: 978-0-615-22766-5
   ISBN-10: 0-615-22766-X

Shaner, Bill. 2. Christian biography—United States. 3. Near-death experiences—Religious aspects—Christianity. I. Title.

BR1725.S447A3 2009   248'.29QBI09-200010

Printed in the United States of America
9 8 7 6 5 4 3 2 1

Permissions
The poem "Faith" by Patrick Overton is used with his permission. Copyright © Patrick Overton, *Rebuilding the Front Porch of America,* 1997. It was originally found in the book, *The Leaning Tree,* 1976.

Cover Photo Copyright © Cliff Mautner, 1989. Used with permission. For more information, visit www.cmphotography.com.

Cover headline Copyright © 1989, Courier Post. Used with permission.

Back cover author photo by Laura Floresmeyer Seaton

All Bible quotations, New Revised Standard Version

In memory of Sheri Wilson

"Thank you, Lord, for bringing me
where I did not want to go."

~ Nikos Kazantzakis

CONTENTS

ACKNOWLEDGMENTS

THIS BOOK HAS VIRTUALLY DEVELOPED ITSELF. Once I acquiesced to write it, every step along the way has fallen into place. When I needed inspiration, it arrived. When I needed to find a particular person to assist with some facet of production, they appeared. It was as if I just needed to shut up, get out of the way, and do what was required. And I tried to do my best.

I wish to thank everyone associated with the development and production of the book you're holding in your hands. They have all duly been credited somewhere within the pages of the book, but I wish to extend my sincere appreciation for their assistance.

I think, in all of our life experience, when we decide to search for something, God puts people into our lives to assist or direct in the search. I know he has in my particular case. I tend to think of these people as sign-pointers on the side of the road of our experience. They provide the direction for the route we're heading in—whether we realize it or not.

To my brothers Tom, Jim and John: I thank you for sharing this life with me. We have made it up some mountains, but also have been in some deep valleys together growing up. We have all gone our separate ways, yet remained connected to each other. Although we may have different perceptions of those experiences, there are no three other human beings I would choose to share them with, and I want to let you know I love each of you very much.

To the Reverends Sam and Bunny Sewell: I sincerely appreciate everything you have done for me. You were correct. When the student was ready, the teacher(s) appeared.

They started my accelerated process of inner growth shortly after I moved to Florida in 2000 (and lost everything I had at that time). I initially met with them to seek counseling but got so much more. I got nourishment. I got direction. And I needed this to keep going.

To the Reverend Tita Calzada, pastor of Unity Fort Lauderdale: You offered me the chance to explore and expand who I thought I was to become.

Shortly after moving to Fort Lauderdale in 2002, I began to attend her church. She provided many opportunities within the church to develop spiritually. The three years I lived in Fort Lauderdale brought tremendous inner change. It was just a start, however, and I needed to go back into the wilderness a while longer.

To Kelly Bennett, who was yin to my yang for eight years, and for that I am truly grateful: You allowed me (sometimes kicking and screaming) to look at a situation from a different perspective. I may not have always liked what I was looking at, but I could at least consider opposing views, whereas before I would simply dismiss them. You are an incredible person.

Finally, I want to thank my biggest sign-pointer of all, Bob Stein. Without you, I would not have found the key place to launch my journey.

Bob and I have known each other since 1994, when we were introduced through my business partner at the time. This was a time in my life when I had really begun to focus on the true existence of God, getting to know Him, and I was starting to answer the questions surrounding my accident and subsequent miraculous recovery. As I close my eyes and replay the events of our first introduction, I can vividly see Bob looking me in the eyes as if to say, "I am here to assist you." And assist he did.

Bob introduced me to many of the greats of the motivational field at the time, and he reacquainted me with God. We continue to discuss various aspects of my spiritual evolution to this day.

Back in 1999, the still small voice within was urging me to move to Florida (as it had since my college days), yet I kept shaking the calling off. My later choice to come to Florida was due, in part, to a decision by Bob and his family to relocate to Florida one year before me. I remember the day when Bob initially told me he was moving to Florida for a business opportunity; I was upset over the prospect of never seeing my friend again. Less than one year later, I came down to see Bob and his family and, upon arriving in Naples, knew this was where I was supposed to be. I didn't know why. I simply knew I needed to be here. Sometimes you just know that you know. The rest is history, or at least a new chapter. Bob, from the bottom of my heart, I thank you for being you. You have been and continue to be an amazing human being.

INTRODUCTION

GOD SPOKE TO ME. I AM NOT CRAZY. FOR ME, these are two statements of truth. They are the reason for this book, a text that has been germinating in my head for the last eight years. Finally, the still small voice within got so loud that I had no other choice than to put down on paper my predominant thoughts to share my story.

This story is simply God's single point of expression through my life experience. It is the story of overcoming a tremendous physical tragedy. That misfortune launched within me a quest to find out what life is all about—to find my truth, so to speak. This is *not* a book about religion. Instead it's a story about redemption and the associated spiritual lessons learned. And don't we all love stories of redemption?

It has taken me twenty years since the tragedy to do what God asked me to do, which was to share my experience with others. I suppose it should have happened sooner, but I chose to run because I was afraid. Basically, I just wasn't ready. Besides, who was going to believe that God spoke directly to me? Such a reaction is not unlike the biblical story of the prophet Jonah, who ran when God asked something of him. Jonah was reluctant to preach to the Ninevites as God had requested, so he hid from God. But when Jonah was about to drown, God created a miracle and saved him. Like Jonah, I experienced a miracle firsthand. I also received a second chance.

I believe that miracles can happen in people's lives when others simply share their experiences. By withholding our experiences, we fail in a vital human responsibility. I now wish to fulfill my responsibility.

Beautiful Blueprints

On July 11, 1989, I died momentarily during a construction accident in Cherry Hill, New Jersey, when a warehouse I was working on collapsed, burying me underneath the rubble. In a way, it was a symbol of how my life was beginning to change and the cocoon I was entering to transform myself into the creature God had intended me to be.

I believe that miracles can happen in people's lives when others simply share their experiences.

You might say that my life before the accident was constructed much like that warehouse. The blueprint was the envy of many. The design seemed flawless and it appeared to be strong and beautiful. This was despite the fact that my start in life had not been easy. However, I took what I thought was wrong and set out to make the best life possible.

At the time of the incident, my personal blueprint consisted of a life of abundance with enough money to buy all the things I wanted, to find a beautiful woman to share it with, to be in control of my work, my life, my time, and the entire world around me. I had designed the perfect life for myself and found everything I'd ever wanted almost ready for final inspection. I was 31 years old, had a highly successful construction business, and had just met the woman who would ultimately become my wife. I owned every toy I could think of and was ready to purchase more. I wasn't sure how life could be better.

Though I had been enjoying a penthouse view, my world would soon shatter like glass. I discovered that the personal blueprint I had was as flawed as the one for the building that collapsed around and on top of me. I emerged as a man broken. In a flash, all I had built was gone. My life was as unstable as the warehouse we had been constructing.

Fortunately, God pulled me back from death and my friends dug me out of the rubble. But I survived only to be told that I would never walk again.

A Search for Answers

With time, I came to realize that I had to create a new blueprint that would help me rise above my new circumstances. I also realized how fragile my life had been and decided that there had to be more. Then, at the hospital, God spoke to me. He helped me find the strength I needed to pull myself up and begin again.

What did all of this mean? I lived among people who simply accepted their problems, which were not as severe as mine; somehow, I could not. Somehow, I knew it was not my destiny to live the rest of my life in a wheelchair. What made me different? And why was the God that I knew to be an angry, judgmental, and punishing deity taking an interest in me with such loving kindness? He offered me hope, strength, and a deep knowing of how to get my body to function again.

This was not the God I had known as a child. This was not the God I had turned my back on since I was a teenager. It was a God I had to redefine and discover. I knew there was something I had missed about life, and I had to know what it was. My life had to have a purpose that went far beyond what I had previously thought was a perfect life.

I found a new determination within that compelled me to search for the God that had come to me in the hospital, the one who wiggled my toes and pushed me into demanding the therapy that would get me out of the wheelchair, rather than teaching me how to be an invalid. This God brought the right people to me at the right time with the right information, and he set my life in order with miracles greater than I had ever experienced.

In our world, there are those who succeed. There are also those who settle for mediocrity. In my search for the truth—for the answers and the God who had saved me—I found that God was within and had been there all the time. And He is for everyone. Ultimately, we all get to decide how our reality turns out.

While that sounds simple, I can tell you it *is* simple. But I will also tell you that simple and easy are not the same thing. Every thought you have changes your life. Each thought moves you ever so slightly in one direction or the other. When you learn about the laws that govern the Universe, you will discover how to use them to create what you want. God is a loving God, and He wants to give you everything you want without judgment. That means if you want mediocrity, frustration, loneliness, and hopelessness, you will get it. If you want love, abundance, confidence, hope, and peace, you can have that, too. It is *your choice.*

Finding My Soul

On a superficial level, I suppose I could have written a motivational book on how to overcome adversity in a few easy steps. That's what I thought I would do when I first started putting pen to paper. But the Universe had a different interpretation it wanted to bring forth through me. This book details the events of that fateful day in July that ultimately changed the direction of my life. It explains the spiritual truths I've discovered in the years since the accident. One of these truths is that we have a say in the outcome of our lives.

It's how we think about something that develops it into our reality. It is our response to sometimes random events that occur in Natural Law that determines our level of success or failure. These events that I describe led me to find my soul. And what an experience that has been!

I will share what has made me the person I am today—lessons from my physical experiences, as well as the spiritual lessons I've learned as a result. I will show how you can—and how you *do*—create your reality. The lessons I have learned have allowed me to live a life of desire rather than one of fear. You too can live a life of abundance and have everything you desire.

The lessons I have learned have allowed me to live a life of desire rather than one of fear.

Ultimately, I will show you how to seek your own truth. And you won't need to go live on a mountaintop to accomplish this. I didn't. I still have a life to live, things to accomplish, and bills to pay.

This book is an opportunity for you to express through yourself the direction you wish your life to travel. If this book touches one other soul, then I have done my job—and what I have been asked to do. Perhaps that soul is *you*.

PART I
WHAT HAPPENED

"I asked for strength, and God gave me
difficulties to make me strong.
I asked for wisdom, and
God gave me problems to solve."

~ Anonymous

Chapter 1

The Day My World Collapsed

JULY 11, 1989. WHILE IT WAS LONG AGO, I CAN still close my eyes and relive almost every moment. It started out as a typical summer day in Cherry Hill, New Jersey. The humid oppressive weather had broken the night before leaving a beautiful sunny day for working. Anyone growing up or living in the Northeast can attest to the sultry weather a Bermuda high can bring. The opportunities to have a day free of the steamy conditions are an unexpected bonus in July. My company had two construction projects which required immediate attention. The night before, I had split my crew in two and decided to supervise the warehouse construction project myself for the day. My usual tasks could be anything since I had no one to help me run my construction business.

I loved working in construction. The great thing about it is that you can stop at the end of the day and see the progress you've made. Everyone on site witnesses the ground being dug, the scaffolding getting put into place, the walls being constructed, and the building taking shape. Each day, the project gets bigger and what you see on paper literally emerges in front of your eyes. It seems to me to be so much more satisfying than just drawing the structure on paper. Oh, I'm sure designing it is pretty satisfying to the person who does that and then works with contractors to develop a finished product. But for me, the charge comes from the actual physical work of building. It's so much nicer than pushing papers around a desk.

We had been working a steady six days a week on the warehouse project to meet the deadline given to us by the owner. Things were progressing well. I had even convinced the masonry contractor to work on the Fourth of July for a half-day with his crew. We brought out a grill to barbeque after we were finished. I even supplied beer

My response to her was "Yes, I'll be there unless I'm killed or something."

for the guys who came out on a holiday to lend a hand. With an American flag installed above the site, what better way to celebrate our freedom than doing something I absolutely loved? That event set us up to meet our schedule, so on July 11, we were looking like we would make it.

This particular day, wooden roof trusses, with a span of 65 feet, needed to be set on the warehouse-in-progress. A crane was scheduled to be on site at 7 AM to start, with an anticipated completion around lunchtime. I had figured that I could supervise my own people since I didn't have any meetings until 2 PM. The unusual part about the afternoon meeting was that I was scheduled to meet with people I had worked for previously, but this was also to be an introduction to new clients. When I'd confirmed the meeting the night before, my realtor friend asked several times if I was going to be able to make it to the meeting by two o'clock. My response to her was "Yes, I'll be there unless I'm killed or something." Omens … too bad we can't listen to our inner voice more often; we would be much better off!

Detour on a Sunny Day

Though the work was hard, the day progressed uneventfully considering the time constraints we were under. As we approached the setting of the last roof truss, I remember looking at my watch and noticing it was past twelve o'clock. The crane was rented for only a half-day and the driver needed to be at another job that afternoon. If we didn't finish before he left, the next available time for the crane to return to our job site was three days later. After some coaxing and bribing, I got the crane operator to stay one more hour to finish up. I was good at negotiations and always made a deal that was satisfying to both parties. Things were going well, and it felt great to stand there admiring the progress made even just that day.

At approximately 12:30, the crane set the last truss. Three carpenters were on top of the masonry wall of the building, while another carpenter and I were on the ground inside the building. Everyone was working well together to get a roof on the warehouse. I was feeling good about things.

Actually, I deserved to feel proud. I was running my own successful construction business. I was only 31, in great physical shape, had money in my pocket, and was told by many women that my looks were ruggedly handsome—standing more than 6 feet tall with brown curly hair and blue eyes. My life was better than I had ever imagined it would be. I also had a meeting that afternoon that would ensure my future success.

Everything is flowing and this life is exactly what I had envisioned it to be, I remember thinking. *Life is great!*

My thoughts shifted to my work. I turned to give direction to the carpenter standing beside me. He had a pretty good life too. He had been with me for a while and drew a healthy paycheck every week. Looking back, I figure that what happened next must have been fate or an angel looking down on us to limit the devastation. I sent him out to the truck to get more nails so we could brace the last truss to the ground.

As soon as he exited the building, I heard a screeching, twisting noise as if someone were pulling a piece of wood out of a wall. I looked around, trying to find the source of the noise. A piece of broken truss hit me in the face. It knocked me backward. I was hit again in the back and then again by the enormous sections of trusses that were collapsing from above. I had no chance to react. It all was occurring so quickly, I didn't know what happened. I saw wood and masonry flying around me and realized the building was collapsing on top of me. There was nothing I could do about it. I couldn't get out of the way. Although it seemed like an eternity, it happened in a matter of seconds. The blow to my face spun me around, and I was buried immediately under a tremendous amount of weight.

Underneath a Pile of Rubble

I learned from the guys later how quickly everything collapsed. Twelve men worked the site that day. Some were on the ground but most were 16 feet high in the air, on top of the masonry walls. As the walls buckled, those on top were either knocked off or they jumped to escape the collapsing structure. Once the men got over the initial shock of this turn of affairs, they checked to see how injured everyone was and did a quick head count. The only person missing was me. Since I wasn't anywhere outside the structure, the men concluded that the only place I could be was buried beneath all the rubble.

Semi-conscious and largely oblivious to my surroundings, I felt my life force draining from my body. I can recall thinking, *It's not supposed to end this way, not here, not now; at least this wasn't how the end of my life played out in my mind.*

I must admit, however, that for as long as I can remember, I had a thought which would occasionally pop into my mind that something dreadful would happen to me one day. Not an overriding fear, but a tiny, tiny feeling that something *could* happen. And this thought stayed in the back of my mind, even though I'm probably one of the most optimistic people you'll ever meet.

I didn't think about that premonition at the time. Instead, moments after the building collapsed on me, I told myself, "I'm ready to go." The feeling of struggle was fleeting and I succumbed to the thought that my death was *I felt myself rising above the collapsed building and beginning to view the site below.* inevitable. With that, everything became dark and I was enveloped by a bright white light. It was the most secure, beautiful feeling I've ever experienced. I felt warm. I didn't hurt any longer. I was at peace and almost eager to head toward a place where I could experience this euphoria.

I actually began to leave my body. I felt myself rising above the collapsed building and began to view the site below. It was at this point that I heard my name being called. My brother Jimmy, who worked on the crew that day, was searching for me despite his own injuries.

At 5 feet 9 inches, Jimmy was 4 inches shorter than me and the shortest of the four Shaner brothers. But he was built like a fire plug with huge upper arms and chest. He was also covered in tattoos acquired during his military service. Jimmy looked as if he would fit in well with a motorcycle gang. Constantly wearing sunglasses and a bandana, his looks belied his quiet nature. Still, like all us four brothers, he would have died to save another one.

This was Jimmy's turn to follow his heart and find the brother who so desperately needed his help. He was on top of the building when the trusses began to collapse and was knocked off the 16-foot wall. With a damaged knee and banged up ribs, Jimmy got the crane operator to lift him into various parts of the building looking for me. Holding onto the hook of the crane with his hands, he searched the wreckage to find me. Without his effort, I know I would have been lost in the wreckage. By continually yelling my name, Jimmy kept my conscious mind from slipping away and helped to keep me alive.

Riding the crane and directing the operator, Jimmy finally found me bent in half under a huge pile of debris. He had the wherewithal to place the hook of the crane on a truss and got the heavy weight off of me before I suffocated. Risking his own life, not knowing if the shifting weight would cause further collapse, he saved my life at least for the moment.

Moving in and out of consciousness, I could barely open my eyes, as they had been virtually swollen shut by the force of the wood hitting my face. I was now bent over in a 45-degree position with my arms twisted through debris almost as if I had been crucified in a sitting position.

Paramedics Work to Save Me

As I came to a little more, I heard fire trucks and emergency vehicles arriving on site. At this point, I had been buried for almost half an hour. The sirens grew louder, and all I could think was: *I'm going to get out of here. I am not going to die!*

I still couldn't get my legs to move when the paramedics arrived to assess the situation. As the paramedics reached me,

I saw the seriousness in their faces. I knew things didn't look good for my condition. My left leg was broken off above my ankle although it was still somewhat attached. I felt hope for my recovery when I heard them call for a chopper so I could be medivacked to the nearest trauma unit once I was extracted.

I felt a sense of relief, believing that I would heal from this accident. Extracting me from the rubble was going to take a little time, though. The ground was unstable and dangerous for anyone trying to cross it, and the debris teetered on itself. Firemen secured the rubble as best they could while the paramedics tried to stabilize my injuries.

Although I've always thought of myself as a fortunate person—I tend to look at the glass as "half-full"—I have had a lot of misfortune in my life. So I often just consider that life is never fair; what counts is how you deal with the misfortunes and move on. Even so, none of this would compare with, or prepare me for, the feeling of being paralyzed. Some *I was indeed paralyzed and could not move anything in my lower body.* things are so basic that we take them for granted; but when one of those basics, such as the ability to walk, is taken away from you, you notice. I can honestly say I was more afraid of not being able to walk again than I was about dying.

As the sirens seemed to quiet, the paramedics radioed back to the truck for the equipment and began to move debris around. Two of the paramedics held me while other rescuers cut me out of my crucified position. I was indeed paralyzed and could not move anything in my lower body. Placed on a backboard, stuck with way too many needles, I began thinking, *It can't get much worse, can it?* Yes it could.

I would not be allowed to have pain medication. "You have to be evaluated at a hospital and we're going to get you to one as quickly as possible so stay with us. Any meds could affect that evaluation. Do you understand?" one paramedic told me. It would be quite some time before I could get anything for the pain.

"No pulse in the left foot," the other paramedic stated.

His partner responded, "We need to set that broken leg then. We need a pulse before we move him or the leg will have to be amputated."

Though my back was broken, the paramedics warned me that I would never feel excruciating pain like when they set my leg in place. They knew what they were talking about! I was told to start screaming while they pushed the leg back together in order to get a pulse. I have never felt anything like that and would not wish the feeling on my worst enemy.

Once my leg was secure, I was extracted from the building and put in an ambulance to drive one block where a helicopter was waiting. The lights and sirens heightened the experience and I found that I was unable to focus my mind. I just kept repeating to myself that I didn't know what was happening and how it couldn't be real. I felt as though I had entered a place where I was far out of control and I didn't know how to get back.

The doors on the ambulance opened and the paramedics pulled the gurney back out into the daylight so I could be brought to the chopper. Every movement caused a wave of pain to cross my body. They were trained to balance compassion with urgency. Their movements were swift, deliberate, and smooth. Though I felt hardly a jostle, those I did feel were excruciating. I was placed in the chopper and the only thought going through my mind was that I couldn't believe this was happening. One minute I was on top of the world and the next I was under the rubble. I had always wanted to ride in a helicopter, but I thought I would be sitting in a seat enjoying the view. What a way to mess up your day.

The Trauma Hospital

The helicopter ride to the trauma unit was no more than 15 minutes, but I can remember the flight nurse shouting to the pilot to get us there as quickly as possible. I wanted this to be over, to be unconscious and out of the inevitable surgery. I wanted to be in a soft bed with this pain a distant memory.

I can't do this … I have a meeting. Who will run my business? I wondered. I immediately reassured myself, *I'll be back on the job in a couple of weeks, in casts maybe, but the job can wait till then. My clients will understand.* I wished it were two weeks later and I could function again.

I felt the chopper descend and heard the paramedics get ready to move me again. We landed on the roof of Cooper Trauma Hospital in Camden, New Jersey. The facility's doors opened and the staff from the hospital was ready to help get me inside. They seemed a little rougher than the ambulance guys, or maybe the pain was getting less tolerable. I couldn't see very well, but my sense of hearing was at an all-time high. I was pulled out of the chopper and put onto a gurney, then taken to a rooftop elevator and down toward the emergency room of Cooper. On the way to the ER, the lights, the noise, and the pale-blue ceiling all flashed by so fast with sounds seeming to bounce off everything.

The emergency room was at a standstill; every doctor and nurse awaited my arrival. Immediately I was probed and pricked everywhere. Doctors and nurses rushed around so fast I couldn't keep track of who was who and what they were doing. They asked so many questions, but I couldn't focus enough to communicate well. I couldn't tell them specifically where it hurt because my entire body was racked with pain; still no painkillers.

From the ER, I was taken for an MRI to determine the extent of my spinal injuries and to look for head trauma. Once an overall MRI evaluation was completed, I was gurneyed back to the emergency room for more x-rays. Then I had to return for more MRIs when the location of my back fracture had been pinpointed. Every time I was moved from a table to a gurney and visa versa, the pain was incredible and soon made me nauseous.

By now, it was approaching 4 PM and the trauma surgeons were on their way to Cooper to prepare for surgery. I was finally able to receive some painkillers as I awaited a trip to the operating room. I remember being in pre-op, moving in and out of consciousness because of the drugs. I saw my brother Jimmy, who refused to get any medical treatment for his own injuries until he knew I would be okay. My other brother John was working at a different project but rushed to the hospital when he found out what had happened. He made it to the hospital shortly before I was taken into surgery.

At one point, I gained consciousness and saw a priest hovering above me, giving me last rites. Having always been blessed with a strong will to survive, I tried to get him to stop because I didn't intend to die. But I couldn't move my arms to wave him away. So in my mind, I blocked him out and felt a fire inside that was going to heal me and prove him wrong.

Go help someone who is really dying and leave me alone, I thought, *because your work here is useless.*

Family Dynamics

Probably the hardest part of the ordeal was thinking about how this would affect my parents. My mom and dad were retired and lived about two and a half hours from my own home. I was the oldest son, and as the years passed, I had evolved into almost a parental role, with my parents becoming my children. You know, that's the funny part about life. You're born and everything is black and white with your parents; in other words, you know what is expected of you. However, in my situation, it was an odd sort of black and white.

My dad was a functional alcoholic, while my mom was an enabler. Dad worked very hard to provide for us, but when he got home and started drinking, you never knew what was going to happen. Uncontrolled screaming or fits of rage could occur at any moment. Once it started, it would generally escalate. Weekends were even worse. Once that first beer was opened, and that was usually before noon, you silently waited for the time bomb to go off. I looked to my mom for protection, and when that didn't come, I knew it was up to me as the oldest son to act as a sort of buffer for my three younger brothers. I learned early on to shut down and go within to control my environment. That was the only way I could feel safe.

When I got out of the house and started college, I saw how many gray areas existed in situations. Life wasn't just black and white. I decided to continue using it to my advantage and never looked back.

After I finished school, I started my own independent life and tried to limit the contact I had with my parents whenever possible. Then as I got even older, and so did my parents, the dynamics of our relationship started to change. They began to turn to me for advice, and I took on the role of their parent. In some situations, responses to their requests become black and white when dealing with them. I would tell them what to do rather than show them options they may have had.

My being incapacitated was going to be a whole new experience for all of us. I was going to have to act on an interpersonal level with them. We were forced to enter a whole new relationship; one I wasn't sure how to handle. I highly suspected that it would not necessarily be on my terms only, but somewhere in the middle. I didn't feel that I could give them much; they had to take some responsibility and some control. Whether I liked it or not—whether *they* liked it or not—our relationship was going to shift.

In any event, my dad had retired four years earlier, and my parents had moved back up to the area where they were originally from. Some friends from Dad's working days were visiting with them when the hospital called. My mom was concerned that I was injured, but they didn't realize the seriousness of the situation. Mom's sister, who was a nurse, lived about a mile from my parents. My mother called to tell her of the accident and to say that they were going to drive down. When my aunt heard I had been medivacked to a hospital, she knew it was extremely serious. My aunt and their brother, who lived nearby and happened to have taken the day off work, immediately picked my parents up and brought them to see me.

As my parents were driven to the hospital, I awaited surgery and thought about my family. I began to realize that my parents did the best they could raising us. I didn't think so going through it, but I now understood. I am the man I am today because of my dad—and in spite of him. Funny that I thought about this then; I guess that was one more reason to live. Who would take care of them? How would they survive without me? How would my family get by? It was too soon to leave them all to fend for themselves. Survival was my only option. I had to be there and I wanted to be there. I wanted to grow old with my family. A shift or not, they still needed me, and I would not let them down.

13 Hours in Surgery

The trauma surgeons came in to tell me their plans and to have me sign some releases. I was so injured that I could only put an X were I was supposed to sign my name. I was told that the vertebrae L-2 in my lower back had been fractured and that they were going to have to do a spinal fusion. The surgeons were going to attempt to reattach my partially severed lower leg, but there was a 50 percent chance it would have to be amputated. The bones above my ankle had completely broken in two and pierced through the skin. Only tissue and skin were holding my foot in place. I pleaded with the doctors to leave my leg on at any cost.

I knew that if the leg were still attached, I had a chance that I could walk again. I told myself that I would not be paralyzed for long. I was going to look normal, act normal, and feel normal. I wanted that clear from the start. I wasn't going to take the easy way out, and neither would the medical team that was putting me back together.

When I was taken to an operating room, I saw an anesthesiologist dressed in the full blue hospital gown, hat, and mask. I heard the obligatory "You will be going to sleep. Just start counting backwards from ten and you'll be out before you get to …"

I woke up sometime the next day in the recovery room and found that I had spent 13 hours in surgery. To replace bone removed from my spinal column, doctors took bone from my hip to insert into my vertebrae. My leg was reattached using a series of plates and screws to keep everything in place. The doctors' immediate concern was repairing the open fracture of my left leg. In addition to all the hardware installed to hold the leg together, the doctors had to clean the area of the injury. Because of the break in the skin, debris and infection can travel to the fracture location, creating a high risk for infection in the bone. Once an infection establishes itself, it can be difficult to treat and amputation may ultimately become the last resort to stop it.

Two Harrington rods were inserted in my back, with vertebrae L-2 through L-4 fused in order to stabilize the back fracture. The two rods were clipped and wired together, then ratcheted to the vertebrae above and below the fusion. They will stay in for life unless an infection develops or one of the rods breaks.

The Philadelphia area always had a very good reputation regarding its medical community. With so many teaching hospitals available, many students come to the region to learn. I had always made note of this to my friends: "How fortunate we are to live in an area where we could be assisted if it were ever required." Little did I know how much I would need it.

A Short Stay in ICU

As I opened my eyes ever so slightly, the first vision I had was seeing my broken-hearted parents looking down at me. They seemed so much older than I remembered. Although there was a 13-year difference between them—my father was 66 while my mother was 53—they both seemed at least a decade older standing at my bedside. Dad was a strapping man, standing 6 feet tall. He was a hard-working, hard-drinking guy. Seeing him standing at the foot of my bed, he seemed to be a man whose life had quickly caught up with him. Mom was a shorter, stocky woman who was always afraid of doctors, let alone hospitals. She certainly appeared out of her element in the intensive-care ward.

They had lost their only daughter years before and were now faced with the possibility of losing their oldest son. By the looks in their eyes, I knew they were in tremendous pain and having a hard time coping. I wanted to slip back into my role of consoling them. I wanted to reassure them that everything was under control and there was no need to worry.

I felt this way even though my dad and I didn't see eye-to-eye on many things growing up. The thing was that I knew he had an extremely difficult upbringing and that the difficulties had continued on into adulthood with the responsibilities of being a parent.

Dad tried standing stoically, but I saw the grief on his face and the tears he would never let fall. My mother, who had battled health problems for many years, was a basket case. Her tears and the loss she was already feeling appeared unbearable. Unable to speak because of the tubes in my mouth, my only response was the tears streaming down both cheeks.

This was probably the most helpless I have felt in my entire life. Every other obstacle I had ever faced was minuscule compared with this. I had always been able to take care of myself; I never needed anybody. After all, I was Bill Shaner. My life had been a great story, being blessed with street smarts and a successful business—I had it all. Now it was all gone. Just like that—gone. I didn't even have anything left to give to the two people who brought me into this world.

I was the caregiver, not the one who needed to be taken care of. *I am going to get that role back,* I told myself. All that I knew, all that I was had changed. I did not know how to act, how to be—and I was not going to spend the rest of my life in this new world. My parents needed me, my brothers needed me, and I needed myself the way I was yesterday.

My strong will to survive and the fact that I've always been a fighter were evident from my pulling through the surgery. In fact, I was fighting back so well that within two days I was out of intensive care and placed in a regular shared room.

A Visit from a Friend

The next few days, I was in such bad shape that I wasn't remembering much of anything: visitors, nurses, meals, etc. The first visitor I do remember, other than immediate family, was Vince, my best friend.

Vince had been on vacation with his family, and upon their return, he got a voice message and immediately came to see me. I remember the look on his face as he entered the room, where I was surrounded by my three brothers. It was the same look almost everyone had upon seeing me for the first time. Vince and I were tight. Not only did we act like adolescents whenever we got together, which I'm sure his wife, Donna, enjoyed, but I considered Vince family. He was my extra brother. Vince and I said we would always do anything for the other person, and I was going to see if Vince was a man of his word.

He laughed and joked with me. "Man, I can't leave you for just a few days without you getting yourself into a whole lot of trouble. Do I have to stay in town for the rest of my life to make sure you won't go hurting yourself?"

Despite his joking, I saw that familiar look of pain in Vince's eyes that I had seen in the eyes of so many of the people around me. After Vince was in the room for about an hour and we got the crying out of the way, I asked my real brothers to leave Vince and me alone for a few minutes because we had to talk about some things. Once the room cleared, I asked Vince, "Do you remember the times when we talked about helping each other out?" Oh, how this request was going to test the limits of our friendship! "If I'm never going to be able to walk again," I told Vince, "I want you to promise to help me kill myself."

At first, he absolutely refused, and I saw it was going to take some convincing. "Not right away," I assured him, "but some time down the road, at a point of my choosing. It would only be after I knew it was impossible to get better."

We never talked about how it would happen, but I got Vince to give me his word that he would do it. And his word was good enough for me. We cried some more, hugged, and then yelled for my brothers to come back into the room. No other word was ever spoken about it again.

Dire News

Dr. William Iannacone, the trauma surgeon who operated on me and kept me alive, visited on the first day I was in a regular hospital room. He asked how I was feeling. "You know, it's remarkable you even made it through," he said. Then he told me that there was a 99 percent chance I would never walk again, that I would spend the rest of my life in a wheelchair.

Then he told me that there was a 99 percent chance I would never walk again, that I would spend the rest of my life in a wheelchair.

I thought, *Well, that means there is a one percent chance that I will. It's not much, but there is a chance I could be that one percent. Someone is, and that someone can't want it more than me.*

Additionally, Dr. Iannacone explained that there was still a chance my reconstructed leg would have to be amputated if infection set in. Not exactly the prognosis I was looking for, but then, they have to tell you the worst-case scenario. I refused to give up just because there was a chance that things wouldn't go the way I wanted.

Dr. Iannacone then spoke of a wheelchair athlete he had known. He wanted this gentleman to talk to me and get me adjusted to the fact that life as I knew it was about to change. I refused to talk with the man. I remember telling the doctor, "You're wrong with this diagnosis; this can't be happening to me. It's a mistake. I know I'm going to walk again!" Now I don't know how many times Dr. Iannacone has had to break news like this to other patients, but with me he had to be wrong. "You're wrong. You must be wrong," I insisted.

He merely sat there and didn't say a word. How hard that must have been for him! After the doctor left the room, I just lay there, numb; absolutely numb. I was angry and tried to tell myself that it wasn't the doctor's fault. Others had simply taken the news as an excuse to give up, and it was easy to just sit there and let life pull you down. He had never met anyone like me before, and he didn't know how powerful a person can be when he wants to fight back.

I couldn't consider for even one moment that I was doomed to spend my life in a wheelchair. I thought, *I have too much to do in life. Too many mountains to climb to call it quits now.*

The next week was pure misery. I don't know if anyone else ever thought about this, but as a child I had a fascination about what it would be like not to have use of my legs. I can remember wondering what it would be like to be paralyzed.

You don't know. You cannot replicate it. Half your body is just dead weight. *Dead weight!* You lie on your back. You can't move. You can't roll onto your side. You can't do anything. I woke up early each day knowing there wasn't a thing I could do—*nothing.* Not a thing I could do or could think of doing would change anything.

I was in constant pain to the point of being shot up with morphine, and begging for the long, lonely, agonizing day to end so I could try to fall asleep and hope to wake up from this nightmare. But the next day would come and I was once again in the same nightmare. It was life, and it was my life. I am such a control freak that I would try to go without the morphine. But the pain would get so bad that the nurses would inject me, sometimes against my wishes, just to help.

In some bizarre way, I know how a heroin addict feels when he's trying to break his addiction but can't. The only peace I experienced was getting shot up with morphine and the euphoria that followed. Only now, the morphine was causing nightmares when I slept.

A few days later, after I was stabilized, I was taken back into surgery to have a shunt inserted into the main artery controlling blood flow from the legs. Once you are paralyzed, you must be concerned that a blood clot could develop in your legs and travel to your heart, where it could kill you. An incision was made above my collarbone, and the shunt was fed down into the artery in my leg. When x-rays are taken today, it appears that I have swallowed a badminton birdie.

At this point after the accident, a clot didn't seem like a bad alternative. I was getting depressed and began wondering if I really would ever walk again. This confinement was not what I had been born to do. I wanted my life to be different. It had been great. It may not have been what anyone else would have wanted their life to be, but it had been mine, and I wanted it back.

I wanted to have at least some of it back, if I couldn't have it all; I wanted my life to be anything but what it was right now. I wanted to see the end of being in the hospital, but I couldn't get my mind wrapped around how I could change things. I couldn't even get out of bed, let alone get out of that hospital.

How long will it take? I thought. *How can I get from here to anywhere that is better than what is happening to me now?*

From the Darkest Despair

A little over a week into my hospital stay, I encountered the experience that truly changed my life. Late one night I lay in bed unable to get any more depressed than I already was. I emotionally broke down and began to sob uncontrollably, begging God to help me. Now I was raised a Catholic and believed in God, but my beliefs were that He was more of a punishing God than a God of mercy. I wore a cross around my neck in the event something might happen to me, but I would not acknowledge God for the blessings he generously gave me each and every day. At some point, I probably wondered what I had done to deserve what happened to me. But now I lay there begging and pleading for help, for mercy. I must admit, as a non-practicing Catholic, my actual plea was more of a bargain with God. "If you allow me to walk again, I promise to go back to church." Desperate times require desperate measures!

As I finished my plea, I heard a voice clearly say, "Everything is going to be all right."

Here's the amazing part. God actually spoke to me in my hospital room. This was the first time I heard His voice. Even so, I feel now that His presence had already been protecting me. Yes, even though something went horribly wrong at the construction site, unexplainable coincidences started to occur there—for instance, how quickly I was found, how the medics stabilized me without doing any further damage to my back, the helicopter getting me to the trauma unit so quickly, the surgery. I could go on and on. But this was the fist time I heard the voice loud and clear speaking directly to me. As I finished my plea, I heard a voice clearly say, "Everything is going to be all right."

Everything was going to be all right ... I heard it and I knew it to be true. I sighed with relief. Someone else believed it, too! I knew I would walk, and now someone else did, too. I turned around in the darkened room to see who was speaking. There was no one else in the room. There was no one walking past the door in the corridor; yet I had heard an unmistakably clear, strong voice tell me everything was going to be all right.

As soon as I heard this voice, calmness unlike anything I had ever felt came over me. I don't know why, but I knew that I would walk again. I was going to be cured. I was so ecstatic that I couldn't fall back to sleep.

I awoke to the strangest feeling the next morning. *Did I speak with God the night before, or was it another morphine-induced nightmare?* My inner self felt so calm and at peace, as if everything was going to be okay, but I couldn't be sure.

Do I risk saying something to the doctors and nurses and be accused of having an undiagnosed head injury? I wondered. I decided, because I was actually so unsure myself, to maintain a quiet but somewhat confident approach. I told no one. Not family, friends, or anyone I came in contact with. It was much safer; I certainly didn't need the medical staff trying to tell me I was just kidding myself, that it was probably from all the drugs. Or that it happened all the time. No, they weren't going to take this away from me, too.

This inner confidence showed almost immediately. Visitors coming to see me said, "Bill, you seem in much better spirits." The tables had turned to the point that I started to regain some of my inner stability and wound up encouraging family and friends that this situation was going to be all right. I was going to get better. I had always been the person who encouraged others to look past current circumstances, no matter how dire they appeared, and to look toward the good possibilities that always existed. Now one of the people I was busy reassuring happened to be myself.

Support, Flowers and a Special Visit

I was humbled by the attention I received from friends and by the number of people who came to visit. Even people I had not seen in years reached out to me after seeing newspaper accounts from the day of the accident. Others sent flowers. I hadn't seen so many flowers since the last funeral I attended.

The number of flowers had gotten so bad (in a good way) that every day the nurses took some flowers for other patients who didn't have any outside support. Besides, since I couldn't get up and move around, I needed the nurses' help in organizing the vast number of flowers, cards, balloons, and gifts that arrived daily. The nurses had another job in assisting me. I had dated several women, and if one came to visit (and they did), I couldn't have them looking at the cards and questioning me on who somebody else might be. The nurses seemed to enjoy my predicament. They knew I couldn't run away.

But the one woman I really wanted to visit me wasn't anywhere to be found. I thought she could be the one who I would ultimately marry. I found something about Amanda to be so special; I couldn't quite put into words what it was. I missed her and wanted so badly for her to walk into the room. She stood only 5 feet 2 inches, weighed no more than 100 pounds, and sported a Billy Idol haircut. She looked like a person who wouldn't take crap from anyone, but she had a smile that would light up a room, with a figure to match. I guess seeing her there in that moment would have made me feel that I hadn't lost it all. And maybe I wanted to know that it wouldn't make a difference to her if I was in bad shape at that time. Then maybe she would want to stick around until I got better.

Amanda and I had been dating for about six weeks and got along really well. I kept my personal life separate from everything else, and Vince was the only other person who knew she and I were dating. We had a date the weekend before the accident, and I had left my ATM card at home. I had to borrow $50 from her, promising to pay her back the following weekend when we were going to get together. The problem was that on Tuesday I got crushed, and the next weekend came and went. The following weekend also arrived and I was still in the hospital. Nobody knew to contact her.

When Vince finally came to see me, he asked if anyone had called her and then said he would take care of it. I figured she must think I was a creep. Not only had I blown off a date, but I also borrowed $50 and never repaid it. Then my friend would be calling her with this lame story. Vince had some serious convincing to do!

After much consternation, she finally accepted Vince's story and came to the hospital to visit. When she arrived, Amanda looked horrified. I knew I didn't look great, but it was the best I could do. Amanda shared with me that after I blew her off the previous weekend, she told her girlfriend that the only way she would ever talk to me again was if I were in a hospital somewhere. Ha, ha, ha—the joke was on her. Now she *had* to forgive me. She said it herself.

Finally a Glimmer of Hope

I kept my experience of hearing the voice of God a secret from everyone for the balance of my hospital stay. I spent a total of two and a half weeks at the trauma hospital before I was discharged to a rehabilitation hospital. The first hospital had no rehab facility to speak of. After I had been stuck resting flat on my back for two weeks, they took me to a room in the hospital that they said was for rehabilitation. But I don't think they ever envisioned someone hurt as badly as I was surviving long enough to need it.

They had no way to assist someone with such extensive injuries as mine. The best they could do was to strap me to this special bed and mechanically rotate me into a standing position. They told me it would assist in equalizing my blood pressure after being prone for so long. That was the first time I had stood in more than two weeks, and boy did I get dizzy. It felt like one of those rides at the amusement park where they spin you around until you could almost puke and then they stop. We did this on two occasions, and then I would return to my room.

I had the good doctor believing in me! Now I just needed to continue believing in myself.

I couldn't imagine how rehabilitation was going to help me in the new facility, but I was going to find out soon. For some reason, I was sent to get CAT scans twice before my discharge. On my last day, I found out the reason. Dr. Iannacone came to see me one last time. He had authorized the additional testing. I was informed that both CAT scans didn't show any punctures of the spinal cord. Although I previously had bone fragments resting against the spinal cord, Dr. Iannacone was confident that he had removed them all.

For some reason, which medical science is still trying to explain, when the spinal cord is punctured or severed, the paralysis becomes irreversible. Despite these test results, I was told there was still a 99 percent chance that I would never walk again. Yet Dr. Iannacone said he could tell by the look in my eyes that I was going to try to prove him wrong. I had the good doctor believing in me! Now I just needed to continue believing in myself.

Living in the Unknown Zone

Cooper Hospital could do nothing else for me. Medically, I was stabilized as much as I could be for the moment. Now it was up to rehab, and the job ahead of me would be trying to learn how to resume some sort of life.

Those two and a half weeks I had stayed at Cooper seemed like an eternity. I had spent almost the entire time flat on my back. I had been fitted with a two-piece fiberglass body cast. That body cast was the most uncomfortable thing I had ever worn. It covered me from directly under my armpits down to my waist. When I was lying flat on my back, it could be taken off. This cast would remain a part of my life for the next 12 months. That was about the only thing I was sure of at the moment.

Almost everything I had taken for granted in my life and much of my being had been ripped away on July 11 and was gone forever. I was totally in the unknown, a place I had never experienced before. I felt as if I had no control over my life any longer. And now I was on the verge of being sent to a new hospital, a new experience, with greater unknowns and greater challenges—only I never imagined what was about to happen next.

Chapter 2

Rebuilding a Broken Body

THE TRANSFER TO MAGEE REHABILITATION Hospital in Philadelphia, Pennsylvania, was a 30-minute ambulance ride from Cooper. The funny thing is, in the short time I was at Cooper, I had become accustomed to those surroundings. As the ambulance crossed the Delaware River into the city, I was overcome with a fear of uncertainty. My body was weak. I kept fighting depression. How would I adjust there? What if they couldn't do anything for me? What if I was never able to walk out of there?

Once we reached Magee, my gurney was wheeled up to the third floor. This floor was reserved for patients with spinal cord injuries: paraplegics and quadriplegics. An entire floor for people with something in common—something that none of us wanted to be known for. It was shortly after noon when I was checked in and taken to a four-person room.

In my new room, the nurses soon placed me in a wheelchair to bring me down to the second-floor cafeteria for lunch. I was told, "This is the only time staff will help by pushing your wheelchair. It is your responsibility to wheel yourself around. You can practice this afternoon."

I just wanted to get into my bed where I felt safe. Meanwhile, the staff was only doing what they were supposed to do. New patients coming to rehab had to relearn daily tasks. However, when I arrived, I was so weak from lying on my back for two and a half weeks that what was left of me could hardly move. Couple this with the fact that only my upper body worked and that a depression had set in … it could be a formula for giving up if I wasn't careful.

The Aquarium Syndrome

I was about to experience the "aquarium syndrome." Anyone who has ever owned an aquarium will understand exactly what I'm talking about. Whenever you bring a new fish home in a bag, you must let the bag, containing the fish and the water from the store, float atop the aquarium water until there is temperature acclimation. At that point, you release the fish into the tank.

In my particular case, I had an 18-hour period to acclimate. I was brought to Magee in the early afternoon, and that would be my only free day. I had to be ready the following morning to begin my new daily experience. I had no idea how to be in this place. Actions and reactions all had to be learned. I wanted to run. It's hard when you are feeling at the top of your game in life and in one split second are reduced to a helpless invalid. I didn't want to be there, and I didn't want to be like most of the patients I had seen so far.

I felt alone and insecure. Though I didn't want to be like them, I would have to learn so much just to get to where they were. A few weeks before, all this had been second nature; now, trying to make any progress was the hardest challenge I had ever faced.

Later that afternoon, my mom and dad came to see me. Two people who had looked so beaten down at Cooper were once again standing at my bedside. I saw so much pain in their eyes that I felt the weight, the guilt, and the discomfort of the uncertain future pressing down on me. What they must have gone through those past few weeks pulled them down in ways I could not have prevented.

Yet as they sat at the foot of my hospital bed, I knew I had to concentrate on my recovery. I had to focus on myself and resolve my own problems. I just didn't have the strength to be there for them too at that time. I knew that I needed time by myself to just relax and prepare for the next round of therapy. I had always been the type of person who would retreat within myself when I had a problem or crisis, and I'd emerge only when a solution began to take shape. My recovery had to begin with me.

I talked to them about the toll this situation was taking on them and on me. I said, "I need to concentrate on getting better, and I don't think it will be necessary for you to stay down here just to come see me and feel sorry for me." My brothers John and Jimmy were around and able to give my parents any help they might need; however, the truth was that my mom and dad had to get on with their own lives. "It's too much for you to ignore your lives while things pile up at home just to sit and watch me go through all of my own struggles," I told them. I promised that I would update them by phone of my progress as time went by. Frankly, I didn't know how long I would be "incarcerated" at Magee. "I would love for you to visit me maybe in a few weeks when we are all feeling better," I concluded.

The first night at Magee, I cried like a baby. I was so worried about the future, about the unknown.

The first night at Magee, I cried like a baby. I was so worried about the future, about the unknown. I had developed toughness over the years to not be afraid, but this one unfortunate incident changed everything. I didn't know how to live like this. I didn't want to live like this, and I was terrified that this would be my future. My mind said, *If you don't learn how to live this way, you won't ever have to live this way.* My logic said, *If you don't learn these things, you will never get beyond them.*

God, I prayed, *you said that I would be fine. I want to be fine. Help me get to fine. You promised.*

Settling into a Routine

Magee Rehab was set up to handle spinal cord and brain injuries. The medical team was composed of a main doctor assigned to each case along with various doctors in training at this teaching institute. Each patient was also assigned a nurse, as well as a physical therapist and an occupational therapist. A daily routine emphasized the skills each patient needed to learn to function in everyday life from a wheelchair. The first full day here was the start of my new regimen.

All the patients were required to be awake by 7 AM for help with getting dressed and preparing for a daily morning round of doctor visits. Since Magee was a teaching hospital, many times the doctors were followed by their students. On those days, my entire medical history was replayed while I was lying there like a giant guinea pig, sometimes being prodded, poked, or pulled on merely for the amusement of the students. At least that's the way it felt.

After that, an assistant would help me get from the bed into my wheelchair. Then, from that moment on, I was on my own with a schedule to maintain. Once any patient from my floor got rolling, a trip to the elevator and down one flight got us where we needed to be for the entire day. During the day, everything occurred for us on the second floor. And if anyone were found in their room, they needed to have a very good reason for being there—no ifs, ands, or buts. That was the schedule; like it or leave it.

Breakfast was in the cafeteria, followed by physical therapy from 9 to 11 AM Monday through Friday. The physical therapist assigned to me (they each had approximately three to five patients) was a petite little angel named Sonia. She couldn't have been more than 5 feet tall, if that, and had the sweetest, quietest disposition I have ever seen in another human being.

I will speak for myself, as well as for others, when I say I was pretty angry when I first started physical therapy. They would work on stretching our leg muscles to try and keep us patients somewhat flexible. That was followed by different techniques on how to get into a sitting position, how to roll over while lying down, and how to transfer from a seated position into a wheelchair. Sometimes I felt like somebody's pet being trained by a professional.

But Sonia could take the anger being expressed and allow it to dissipate while smiling and bringing a sense of calmness into the situation. She was working on her graduate degree in the same field and felt this was her calling. I could see that it was from the way she treated people. We quickly became friends, and I knew she would assist me in finding answers to whatever questions I had about my recovery.

Physical therapy was followed by lunch, and then patients had to be in occupational therapy at 2 PM. By the time occupational therapy was over at four o'clock, we had a short time to get ready and then wheeled ourselves to the dining room.

I discovered an interesting dichotomy with this whole surreal experience I was immersed in. During meals, we hung out in cliques, as if we were all back in elementary school.

Once dinner was over, we all went back to our rooms in anticipation of visitors. It was the real world coming in to express itself for a few hours. Other than passing in the corridor, or outside on the veranda, we never really had contact with other patients at night. On the occasion we did, it was usually a brief introduction to other patients' visitors because we were always consumed by the people who came to spend time with us.

A New Friend

While at Magee, I became close with a gentleman named Ed. He was a 58-year-old union man who had worked hard all his life. Stocky in build, Ed looked like a man who never backed down from anything. He raised a family, had bought a second home down at the Jersey Shore, was going to be a grandfather in the near future, and had been working toward retirement.

One weekend down at the shore, Ed was helping an elderly neighbor clean up around the house and climbed a ladder to clean leaves out of the gutter. While on top of the ladder, Ed blacked out because of the heat and fell backward. He struck his head on a boat parked in the driveway, breaking his neck and being rendered a quadriplegic. What did he do to deserve that? *Nothing. Absolutely nothing.*

We often talked about that fateful day. Many times Ed broke down, crying uncontrollably. I tried to explain that sometimes bad things happen to good people. He just couldn't understand it. He was putting in his time for retirement and waiting for the day when he didn't have to work anymore. Even with my own situation staring me in the face, I had empathy for that man. I met his wife once or twice in passing, but she was the only one I was introduced to from his family.

Ed and I were tight during the daytime. We met for coffee every morning, and usually ate lunch together and most times dinner, too. Ed sought me out on bad emotional days, and his despair would almost overwhelm me, but I did my best to keep it together for his sanity as well as my own. I think that's why I didn't necessarily want to get to know his wife. Initially, I didn't understand why. I had tremendous compassion for this woman but could not express it. I knew the tragedy she had gone through and how her future had changed in an instant. Yet my own self-preservation did not allow me to express my compassion for others. How do you explain, or for that matter justify, how a man can go from breadwinner to helpless human being in the blink of an eye? But then again, it wasn't up to me to explain. I had my own nightmare to deal with.

How do you explain, or for that matter justify, how a man can go from breadwinner to helpless human being in the blink of an eye?

Finding Determination

Once I figured things out and got to know the staff and patients, I discovered I could get back to my room for a little break during the day. Sneaking back to the room acted like a coping mechanism for me. I would put headphones on, listen to music, and take a break from the insanity my reality had become. In the beginning, they pretty much pushed everyone to conform. But I always got along well with the nurses, so they looked the other way.

Sounds like a pretty good existence, doesn't it? Don't think that for a minute! I went from self-sufficient person, a business owner who so many people depended on, to a broken-down human being who was completely dependent on everyone else for every need. I needed help getting dressed and undressed, help getting in and out of bed, and help taking a shower; nothing was easy and nothing was anything like it was before. Even going to the bathroom required assistance.

Yet, somehow, some way, I wasn't giving up. While I had definite moments of depression and anger, they didn't last long. With the move to Magee, I soon gained a new level of hope that I was going to beat this. I'd had many difficulties in my life prior to this, and I wasn't going to let my current condition stop me either. If I learned how to be in a wheelchair better than anyone, they would be more likely to teach me how to get out of it. If they didn't, I would find someone who would or I would do it on my own. I was determined to get on my feet as soon as possible. I knew I would walk; now it was just a matter of time.

Still, I had much to cope with. For instance, one of the first things the doctors decided was that they would be injecting me every day with Heparin, a blood-thinning medication, to prevent blood clotting, even though I had a shunt installed. The Heparin was injected in my stomach. Therefore, every morning before breakfast, I felt the needle entering my lower abdominal muscles, all for the sake of perpetuating this miserable existence I was becoming accustomed to.

Additionally, my lower abdomen, butt and legs constantly felt like they had fallen asleep. Most paralyzed people have no sensation in their affected areas at all. Since my back fracture was incomplete, the spinal cord was not severed, so I had a numbing sensation all the time.

Also, since I had a numbing sensation constantly, my butt was always sore from sitting in a wheelchair. For paralyzed people, the problem with no sensation is that you must be careful about developing sores on the skin from staying in one position too long. If you can't feel the sores, you might miss them. So, all things considered, I suppose my constant irritation wasn't so bad. It gave me even more hope. I didn't have dead weight; it was more like still weight. I was different and I wasn't going to let the medical staff tell me to give up on my visions.

Coping with Monotony

Five days a week, the exact same routine played over and over until I lost track. Every waking moment was planned out and never varied. My life during the day was only about learning to be a self-sufficient man limited by his wheelchair. Weekends were even worse. No therapy classes to break up the ungodly monotony. The days were long. The nights were worse.

After dinner each night, I was on my own. Visitors were allowed from 6 to 8 PM. I was fortunate that my brothers would visit, and I had a lot of friends who came to see me. Amanda kept coming to visit me, too. I wasn't quite sure at first whether it was pity or she was trying to get her $50 back, but we actually started finding out a lot more about each other and our relationship began to deepen. There are many clichés in life, but the one about finding out who your friends are in a time of need is so true. I was surprised to discover how many people did care about me. I will always remember them. I am overwhelmed and grateful to have had so much support.

When visiting hours ended at eight, the boredom really crept in. With the visitors gone, the hospital was quiet again. There wasn't much to do. I never thought I could watch so much television. I wasn't the kind of guy who sat in front of the TV before, so all of it was new to me. After lights out at 10, I would just lie awake with the TV on. I think I saw every infomercial ever aired during the time I was at Magee. Every computer school, truck-driving school, and every technical school out there had commercials that I knew by rote. Every commercial for attorneys, where they promise to stand up for your rights and get you the money you deserve, played over in my head while I thought that, for all my injuries, I couldn't even sue. It was an accident, and to dwell on blame and try to figure it all out wasn't going to help me with my goals.

Shower night, every other night, broke up the boredom somewhat. Any sense of modesty I might have had was soon swept away. A nurse would come into the room and strip me naked, help me into the wheelchair, and roll me into the shower, where I was left to wash myself and wait to be brought back to my bed. I had help drying myself off and getting back up on the mattress. I then lay there with wet hair, shivering and freezing because my body was so weak.

Before finally falling off to sleep, I prayed that this was a cruel joke, a mistake that wasn't actually happening. Praying that I had enough strength to deal with whatever lay ahead gave me enough strength to make it through the day. Then morning would arrive and the whole vicious cycle started again.

Life Goes On

After breakfast each morning, I had maybe 30 minutes when I could wheel onto a second-floor outdoor deck and look at the skyline of downtown Philadelphia. In the mornings, I sat out there watching the rush-hour traffic go by and I'd feel so angry. It was my only face-to-face connection with what used to be my real life. How could all those people continue on with their own lives when mine had come to a screeching halt?

My disappearance should have caused at least a small ripple in their everyday lives. Was I so insignificant that the world could function just the same every day whether I continued to be involved or not? Well, the world goes on no matter who lives or dies, or gets snatched away and thrown into a wheelchair where he's supposed to happily take it and learn to live that way for the rest of his life. The world doesn't notice, and it keeps on going. Still, those 30 minutes on the outdoor deck each morning actually helped me keep my sanity. The sunshine and fresh air, and viewing the traffic below, allowed me to release some of the anger and resentment that continued to build up inside me.

I heard myself screaming on the inside about how unfair it was that the people below could continue on with their lives while mine was in shambles. I couldn't go to work. I couldn't go home at night. I wasn't waking up to the woman of my dreams. I couldn't experience all the exciting or mundane things these people were living every single day. I still had hopes and dreams I wanted to fulfill. But because of some cruel twist of fate, my life was put on hold.

But it's not what happens to you, it's what you do about it.

I had to figure out how I was going to fix me—how to change my current physical state. It almost wasn't fair, but that's not how I look at things most of the time. Stuff happens to all of us. Some things are worse than others. But it's not what happens to you, it's what you do about it. I've been so fortunate to be able to look at life that way. It still doesn't make the task at hand any easier, but we must forge ahead. We can't look back and feel sorry for ourselves. It's not going to do any good. Besides, if you look over your shoulder often enough, whatever you envision chasing you will catch you.

I knew that, and I had always lived by this theory. But now that I had such severe struggles in life, I found that I had to work harder at remembering to let go, to not get angry, and to find the strength to move on. On some level, I thought that if I let go of the anger, I would give up and acquiesce to life in the wheelchair. I struggled back and forth with the anger and always held onto the thought that God promised I would be all right. Maybe I didn't need the anger to keep working toward getting my body back. I couldn't remain angry at those people down there. They didn't even know me. Besides, I'd never had a thought about what had happened to other people before this. I was too busy being the best construction bigwig I could be to have thoughts of people who couldn't get out of wheelchairs and were suffering.

I knew at some point I might have to figure out what I was going to do if I couldn't walk again. Still, I didn't want to believe it. I would fight with the doctors, the nurses, the therapists—anyone who I could get to listen to me. I insisted I was going to get better. The nurses and therapists pressured me to work at developing wheelchair skills in order to get released from the hospital. But I couldn't even pretend that a wheelchair was okay simply to get out of Magee. I could not and would not give up just yet.

Facing Another Pivotal Test

In talking with the doctors one day, I learned that an EMG test could tell whether I had nerve activity in my lower extremities. If this test was unsuccessful, there would be no chance I'd be able to walk again. Even if the test results were positive, doctors warned, no certainty existed that I might regain use of my legs. There was no certainty that I couldn't either. I was willing to take the chance.

I begged the doctors to give me this test. I promised that if the test results were negative, I would give up the hope to walk again and become the best rehab patient they had. However, if the tests were positive, I would continue to press on to get out of the wheelchair.

The next day, we went into a small room in the hospital. This room contained an exam table and a machine that looked like something out of a science-fiction movie. Electrodes attached to a long needle would be inserted into various muscles in my legs—what was left of them anyway. A noise, similar to a Geiger counter, meant nerve activity was still present. It is my understanding that damaged nerves can regenerate themselves at the rate of one inch per year. And after five years, whatever nerve regeneration took place would be the limit of what a patient might expect.

I was positioned on the table and warned that the needle was going to be "uncomfortable." What great terminology the medical community uses so you don't just get up and leave. The needle was inserted into my right thigh, and it hurt like hell, but you know what? The machine made noise! And that was all I had hoped for. But the doctors said it meant nothing. The needle was then inserted into my right calf. The lesser amount of flesh to go into, a more intense feeling of pain, but there was still a response from the machine. The doctors then inserted the same needle behind my right ankle and a similar result occurred. We then duplicated the procedure down the left side, producing an equal level of pain—and matching positive results!

I would have danced if I could, but that would have to wait until I got my legs to work again. Even though I knew I would walk again, the doctors maintained that the test didn't mean anything. I had no other sign that muscle activity was occurring, and my legs were getting smaller and smaller because of muscle atrophy. But I knew that it did mean something. These new results meant that there was more hope than we had suspected.

The clues were mounting. Now I would need to find a way to work these muscles if I was going to walk again. In the short-term, it actually would have been easier for them if I had just given in and followed the routine of the stuck-in-this-stupid-wheelchair-forever patient. But I chose the path that would take me back to being myself, to the Bill I remembered and longed to be once again.

If God had really spoken to me in the hospital, then the results from this latest test were a sign from above. This was an affirmation that I was going to be healed. Yet the doctors didn't get it. When the two of them came into my room the next morning, I was waiting for them. They still tried to convince me that the test was not necessarily a reliable indicator of what the future held. They followed that with some other medical mumbo-jumbo, but it didn't matter. I knew what I knew. It was my unshakable belief. Well, kind of. I had an underlying knowing that I was going to walk again, but no physical signs that it was going to happen anytime soon. I would not let them take away the feeling that I had. The machines only confirmed what I already knew.

Even if the doctors were saying the results didn't mean a thing, the test meant something, and I was going to find a way to walk with or without their help. In fact, the moment I got back onto the second floor, I wheeled myself into physical therapy and grabbed Sonia to talk to her for a moment. She thought it was odd that the doctors gave me little hope because of the results. I remember that Sonia insisted she wasn't a doctor, but she thought the results from the tests were encouraging. *So did I.*

A Pass to Go Home

No one was allowed to leave the premises—not even out in front of the hospital—without a pass. After about a month of the same boring day-to-day routine, the doctors felt I was stable enough to have a weekend pass to go home. Even though it was a weekend pass, I was still required to go back to the hospital Saturday night; then I could leave again Sunday morning for the day. My weight had stabilized, and I was beginning to make progress in handling a wheelchair. At the same time, the paralysis in my legs had taken its toll. They were reduced to half their thickness with my left leg still in a cast, and I still wasn't sure if that leg would have to be amputated at some point. Also, we didn't know whether the left leg would work if I ever had the opportunity to regain muscle control in my legs.

This chance to get out into the real world triggered a rush of feelings. It was freeing, exciting—and scary.

This chance to get out into the real world triggered indescribable feelings. It was indescribably freeing, exciting—and scary. Magee had become my home. I was used to those surroundings. As sad as this sounds, I felt safe there.

The first Saturday, I was getting ready to leave and I didn't feel quite right. I attributed it to nervousness. The doctors looked me over as they did every day and found I had developed a low-grade fever. They wanted me to wait for a different weekend to take the pass; however, as soon as my brother Jim arrived, we left the hospital and headed for home.

My anxiety subsided, and I was ready to return to something that would remind me of what my world had been like before this all happened. It was the real world. I was ill, but happy.

While I was at my own home for the first time since July 11, I got to see Mom and Dad again, as they had traveled down to see me. Amanda even came to spend the day. I was propped up in a chair and sat fairly still for the day. I could not do much else. It was almost like being in the hospital, but I could look around, close my eyes, and remember the sounds and the smells. For a moment at a time, I could be myself as I knew that person who I had been. It didn't last, though; my body still ached and the medication began to wear thin. As the hours passed by, I felt more and more ill. My body started to ache continuously. I couldn't eat and finally asked to be taken back to my bed at Magee.

The ride back was horrible. Every bump we encountered was unbearable. I couldn't stop aching. My body hurt so badly.

A Temporary Setback

Two nights later, Amanda snuck in, late after visiting hours were over, to see how I was feeling. I remember I felt so sick that I didn't even want to see her. I always wanted to see Amanda, and to not want her there should have told me something was wrong. She immediately noticed I had turned yellow and rushed out to get a nurse.

A doctor was brought in and he called for the nurses to draw blood. The results came back the following day. I was diagnosed with what the doctors would call "non-A, non-B hepatitis." I had lost more than half my blood at the accident scene because of the severely broken left leg. Blood transfusions after the accident introduced the hepatitis virus. I was now yellow and every inch of my body hurt. My hair even hurt!

I think at this point I was truly ready to give up, yet again ready to throw in the towel. Maybe the cards were actually stacked against me; maybe I wasn't supposed to get better. I actually thought I would be better off dead than to continue getting beaten down while I was trying so desperately. If God was going to make everything all right and put my body back together, why was he making it so hard? Why was I facing one problem after another?

The doctors and the physical therapists thought I should give up and learn how to be a good wheelchair victim. But to me, this didn't make sense. Since I didn't die on the day of the accident, I believed that I was supposed to get better—and regain the use of my legs. I just knew it. But why was there no progress?

Getting a "Toe Hold"

A few days after the doctors got the hepatitis under control, I awoke and pulled the covers off my feet. As I did every day since the accident, I tried to get my feet to move without any success. Except this day I got the little toe on my right foot to wiggle, ever so slightly. I pulled the call button over my bed to summon the nurses and showed them the toe movement.

I got the little toe on my right foot to wiggle, ever so slightly.

They went and got the doctors. I showed the doctors as well. "It could be involuntary," they said.

Yeah, right! I focused on my right foot, summoning it to move, and the little toe responded. Involuntary? *Please!*

A few days later, I was able to get the same response from the little toe on my left foot, which was still in a cast. I was ecstatic. The nurses smiled. The doctors were perplexed. It didn't matter. I knew I would regain use of my legs.

After the little toe on each foot moved, the physical therapists were told to work with me to try to regain muscle use in my legs. A dolly was placed under each leg, and while I was lying on my back, I would try to move each leg back and forth as if I were making a snow angel. It was more difficult than I ever knew it could be to move them. Though the weight was very light, doing this movement seemed like an impossible task. But then each bit of progress gave me hope for the next. I wasn't going to stop. I was going to walk no matter what it took!

We started out with no weight on each dolly. But as I improved, they added small incremental weights to each side. For two to three hours each morning, I would wield these dollies back and forth. I was so focused on getting the use of my legs back that I convinced the occupational therapist I saw every afternoon to allow me back into physical therapy to keep building my legs up. I did this for weeks to strengthen my legs.

Paralysis can do incredible damage to the body. To be able to move a little toe so slightly was such a joyous feeling, but I didn't know what lay ahead in regaining my old physical form. No one even knew if it was possible for me to get it back. I was determined to find out, no matter what the cost. I was becoming the paraplegic Rocky Balboa—without drinking raw eggs, of course. My left leg was still casted and pinned together. Doctors didn't know how it would respond to bearing my body weight if I got to the point of standing up. I could only cling to hope.

Each level of therapy was initially exciting, but then some level of boredom set in. One can only spend so many hours making snow angels. I felt as though I was easily doing the exercises, and yet I was being told that I had to keep doing them because I wasn't ready for the next step. While I felt like I was treading water, I continued to exercise in whatever way they would let me so that eventually I would be able to move up. If I stopped, I would slide back and the medical team would stop the process altogether. It was much better to be bored than to stop.

Time Moves On

By now, July had turned into August and August into September. The days passed on and the weekend passes allowed me to keep my sanity. As much as I enjoyed getting out for the day, in some bizarre way it was so nice to get back to the hospital at night. I hated the hospital, all that it was, and all that it represented. Still, it had become my safe zone, my home. I've read about prisoners studied after their release, and in many cases, they would not venture far from where they were even in freedom because they had become accustomed to their former tight surroundings. I kind of felt the same way.

The doctor asked, "How are things going?"
"I can move my legs!" I told him proudly.

Magee had become my norm. No matter what was happening on the outside, I felt safe and secure there.

Sharing My Progress

Just before Labor Day, I had an appointment to return and see Dr. Iannacone. It would be our first meeting since my discharge from Cooper Trauma. My brother Jim took me for the checkup.

I remember being wheeled into an exam room and then being greeted by Dr. Iannacone. We exchanged pleasantries and I thanked him for what he had done for me. Then, after he had turned away to review my file, the doctor asked, "How are things going?"

"I can move my legs!" I told him proudly.

A brief moment of silence followed before he blurted an accidental incredulous expletive. He dropped his pen onto the counter, spun around with a smile on his face, and said, "Show me!" His excitement over this news was contagious.

We both laughed and I leaned back a little in my wheelchair. I was able to flex a little muscle on the top of each thigh. He was ecstatic. So was I.

"You know," he said, "everyone tells me they are going to get better. So few actually do. I never wanted you to get your hopes up only to break down later and blame yourself." He beamed at me. "But you ... I saw such determination in your eyes. Well, I knew if anyone was going to walk again, and if there was any way possible, it would be you!"

I had wanted so much to prove him wrong, that I knew this day would come. I don't think there was too much more of an exam. We both knew how things were turning out.

Visiting the Jersey Shore

Labor Day weekend, my brother Jim took me down to the beach in Ocean City, New Jersey. The shore holds a fascination for me, and I have always loved going to the beach ever since my first visit as a seven-year-old. As a child, we never took vacations. The highlight of every summer, other than not having to go to school, was a daytrip to the ocean with my mother and, at the time, two brothers.

I grew up in Levittown, Pennsylvania, an hour-and-15-minute drive to Seaside Heights, New Jersey. One of my earliest memories is my mother announcing a few days prior, "We're taking a daytrip to the shore!" For me, this trip held the same magic as Christmas. After experiencing it for the first time, the anticipation of a shore trip always kept me awake all night (just like when I anticipated Santa's arrival).

As a child, this day at the beach was always the best day all summer. It was so exhilarating. It didn't matter how cold the ocean was. A day of riding the waves and playing in the sand did wonders for my soul, even as a kid. It was on this day that all was well with my world. I never wanted the day to end. During the long rides home with sand in every conceivable crevice, the taste of salt remaining on my lips, and a varying degree of sunburn, I was still able to experience the feeling of waves crashing over me. Even that night in bed, I slept so soundly reliving the motion of the waves. Those days at the beach represented what I wanted my life to be—happy and carefree with no worries or concerns about tomorrow.

The roar of the ocean, the call of the seagulls, the smell of the shore air—I drank it all in as if I were experiencing it for the first time.

Water has a calming effect on me. Whether it is the ocean, a lake, or a river, I have always felt recharged around water. The ocean was always the best, though. I suppose on some subconscious level that is why I have never lived more than an hour from the shoreline. Even when I vacation as an adult, a beach has to be part of the package.

When Jim suggested the possibility of getting out of Magee on a day pass and heading to the ocean, it felt like I was reliving my childhood. The night before, I mentally "tossed and turned" in anticipation. (Physically, I couldn't actually toss and turn, as I was lying in my usual prone position.)

As we headed out the next morning, I felt the excitement of what was going to happen mixed with some trepidation. I worried about what people would think when they saw me in a fiberglass bodycast being pushed around in a wheelchair. That represented, for me, that I was not normal or whole as everyone else seemed. But for a chance to visit the beach, it was a risk I was willing to take.

Amanda came along on the trip. Our destination beach was only an hour-and-a-half drive from the hospital. Still, sitting in a car with the fiberglass bodycast on was a pain. But getting to the shore was well worth the discomfort.

Once we got into the shore town of Ocean City, New Jersey, I felt as if I were returning to be healed. The roar of the ocean, the call of the seagulls, the smell of the shore air—I drank it all in as if I were experiencing it for the first time. Despite how frequently I had been to the ocean, this time was different. I was enjoying it in a way I never had before.

As we wheeled up onto the boardwalk, all was definitely well with my world. The crashing of the surf, the sun radiating down on me, the tantalizing aroma of pizza from the shops, and the sounds of people playing arcade games resonated within my long-tested soul. The trip transported me to the innocence of a seven-year-old experiencing the shore for the first time. Part of me was saying to the world that I was back and wasn't giving up. I was just there recharging my batteries.

I don't think I have ever appreciated the beach as much as that day, when everything from my past seemed a distant memory. Nothing felt the same, especially the stares from people who probably wondered what had happened to me. But when I closed my eyes and took in the smells, the breeze, and the bright sun on my skin, I felt like I had always felt when I was there. Of course, after spending two months in the hospital and finally getting out into the bright sun, the tops of my legs and shoulders and my face got quite sunburned. Still, it felt so good that I would have done it again; it was well worth the pain. Besides, pain and I were so well acquainted at this point that a little sunburn pain would merely remind me where I was when I got it.

Unnecessary Alarm

We arrived at Magee later that evening. After everyone left, I wanted to get a shower to remove the salt and the sand from my tired and beach-worn skin. The regular staff knew I was going to the beach for the day, but by the time we got back they were all gone. One of the staff on duty helped me get ready and wheeled me into the shower room. Sitting in a body cast, naked and in a wheelchair, I enjoyed letting the shower rinse off my body. I just sat there with my eyes closed reviewing the incredible day that had recently ended.

A few moments later, a substitute nurse working on the floor came in to check on me. When she saw the sunburn on my legs, she assumed I had burnt myself with the hot water from the shower. Without even giving me a chance to explain the situation, she screamed, turned off the water, and ran out of the room to get help. Within moments, several people had descended into the shower room thinking they were going to have to deal with a burn patient.

They grabbed my wheelchair and spun me around. They urgently discussed what to do until the doctor arrived, talking simultaneously and drowning each other out. I kept trying to explain that I had been at the beach that day, but no one listened. And no one seemed to care that I was sitting there naked, wet, and quite frankly a little chilly as I attempted to clarify things.

We had to wait several minutes for a doctor to arrive. The room became quiet and the staff moved aside to let the doctor get close enough to examine my red, naked body. He asked what the problem was and everyone started chattering again. He quieted them down and let me talk.

I calmly explained, "I was at the beach today. If you'd check the table next to my bed, you'll find a couple boxes of saltwater taffy. It's the kind you can only buy at the Jersey Shore."

The doctor then made his diagnosis: I had been at the beach that day and I could now complete my shower in peace.

It still was a great day. And I got to relive it every time I had to tell a staff member that my red skin was not a burn from the shower. I had been to the beach!

That night, after the shower incident, I rested in bed reliving the day at the shore like I had as an innocent child. I slept soundly, while my imagination allowed me to experience the waves of the ocean crashing over the top of me. I knew then that, at some point, I would walk again so one day I would actually be able to experience the waves for real.

Preparing to Walk

After Labor Day, my therapy began to include standing at a three-sided railing. I would stand for only a few minutes at a time so my legs would become used to bearing my weight again.

This was the first time since July 11 that I could stand on my own two feet. It lasted only about two minutes, but this was a start—a glorious two minutes that gave me an incredible amount of inspiration. If I could stand for two minutes, I would soon be able to stand for five and then 10. My objective was to begin working on balance again. I didn't realize how much our leg muscles control balance.

This was the first time since July 11 that I could stand on my own two feet.

In the early days of therapy when I was first at Magee, they would seat me on a padded table bench. To develop my abdominal muscles for balance, they tossed a beach ball for me to try to catch. I had to take my hands off the bench and rely on other muscle groups for balance. When I fell over, they picked me up to try again and again until I became proficient at it.

By this time in early September, I had been fitted for fiberglass leg braces that would provide support during my early attempts at walking. But I was ready to go, and these braces were at least a week away from being manufactured. I couldn't wait; I had a life I wanted to return to as soon as possible. I remember asking Sonia, "What else can we do?"

Sonia was such a sweetheart, a real gem. "We have a couple pair of old leg braces around here somewhere. I'll look for them," she told me. And she did.

The next day when I came to physical therapy, a set of ungodly looking braces lay next to my work table. I was so excited that I could hardly wait to get these beauties on. They were a key to getting back to my life. I didn't care how they looked or how I looked in them. Sonia had even installed new Velcro strips on the braces to make them more secure.

My initial reaction was that they looked and felt like Herman Munster boots. Big and bulky, just like the footwear seen on Fred Gwynne in that 1960s TV sitcom. No matter. It was time. All the dreaming, praying, begging, and hoping was about to come to fruition. It was time to walk!

They secured a strap around my waist for balance and to hold onto me if I fell. Initially, two therapists were to assist me with walking. With one therapist on each side, they would hold the strap to control direction, balance, and support. They secured the leg braces and got a walker for me to hold onto during my attempts. Now, finally—after more than two months of agony—I was about to take my first step. Boy was I scared! Now was the moment of truth. Could I actually do it? Was this really going to be the beginning of getting my life back?

I can't fail, I thought, *I can't fail. I was not going to prove* **them** *right.* **I** *was right. I was going to walk again, and these were going to be my first steps. After this, it would be easy.*

Walking My Talk

Ever since I arrived at Magee, I had been trying to motivate other patients on the third floor. "There is hope for everyone," I'd say, "even me. No one should give up. No one should *ever* give up."

Now, here I was, with all the other patients and therapists gathered around to watch me to see if the talker could "walk the walk" with the help of the leg braces. I slowly got up into a standing position, steadied myself in the walker, and took my first step—then a second one. I think I actually got about half a dozen steps in before I needed to sit and rest.

Why me? Why did I get the opportunity to walk again while many others in similar situations would not?

I thought of the old saying about never forgetting how to ride a bike. It's not quite the same as walking again. The room erupted with applause from the other patients and therapists for what I had accomplished. *It was a miracle.* Then again, I had known this day would happen since the night God spoke to me and told me it would be all right.

Yet there was a side of me that was sad and confused. *Why me? Why did I get the opportunity to walk again while many others in similar situations would not?* That question weighed on me for a long time. I was happy that it did happen for me, but I wanted to know how and whether I could help others achieve the same success I was experiencing. This had to be a miracle that others could access, too.

I have really come to believe that sometimes inexplicable things happen to each of us in the course of our lifetimes. The Bible says that the rain falls on the just and unjust equally. It's not that God abandons us, because I believe the exact opposite is true. In my situation, God put people in place the day of the accident to save my life. The paramedics on site that horrible day placed me on a gurney with such precision and care that there was no further damage to my spine. Had I been moved in a different way, I could have been paralyzed for life. The same is true of the trauma surgeons at the hospital, who performed more than 13 hours of surgery to save my life, and the therapists who worked with me, especially after I regained some use of my legs.

Some things in life cannot be explained, and the question *"Why me?"* provided an opportunity to look inward and find that my life is my own. My choices are the ones that are the best *for me*. Others may make different choices that are best *for them*. The only tragedy is when someone merely accepts what happens to them as fate and dwells in the misery of life. They become what they don't want rather than choosing to make a life they do want.

No one outside of the therapists and other patients saw my progress during the day. By the time visiting hours started, I would either be sitting in my wheelchair or lying in bed, exhausted from the events of the day. So, after practicing walking for a few days, I convinced Sonia to allow me to borrow the temporary braces for the evening so I could show Amanda and my brother Jim that I was capable of walking. I sat in my room anxiously awaiting their arrival.

When they finally got to my room, I said, "I have a surprise for you! Jim, take my arm and help me stand up." He did. I took hold of the walker to steady myself and took a few steps. Amanda began to cry at the sight of the miracle. Her excitement was infectious, and soon the three of us stood there with tears streaming down our cheeks. I sat back down, exhausted but filled with emotion. We laughed and joked about how I was going to be running the Boston Marathon the next year.

A Few Moments in the "Real World"

The walking got a little better each day. It progressed to the point where I was allowed to practice shuffling back and forth on my own with a set of parallel bars for support. Every once in a while, my legs would give out under me. The bars caught me, though, so I never hit the floor or had to worry too much about causing more injuries. I would stand back up, rest for a few minutes, and then continue.

In addition to walking a straight course inside, I had to learn how to use stairs all over again and then work my way toward going outside to trudge along in city conditions. It all happened gradually, step by step.

The first time the door actually opened and I walked outside, I almost collapsed from the excitement. It was a day that I had dreamt about since the moment of the accident, or sometime shortly after I discovered I was not going to die. It was a bright sunny day, and the sunshine felt good on my face. I imagined that I had the same sense of accomplishment that Rocky Balboa had from his boxing training, except I knew I wasn't ready for the Art Museum steps just yet!

I want to do it all on my own, I thought. I just don't know if I can.

I didn't walk far, but it was far enough to bring every emotion I ever had to the surface. I was excited, inspired, and scared to be back, if only for a few minutes, in the "real world."

No one kept me from reaching my goal, I thought, *and I am feeling the sun on my face as I walk out of the Center and down toward the street. What a glorious day!*

Heading Home

By the beginning of October, I thought I was becoming a pro at this thing they called "walking." Then came the news I had hoped for but dreaded. I was well enough to be discharged from the hospital. I was so happy, yet so scared. I would have to learn to function in society on my own all over again. I would have no therapists, no nurses, and no doctors to care for my every need.

I want to do it all on my own, I thought. *I just don't know if I can*. It had been so long, and I had wanted this day to come. Now that it was here, I wasn't so sure I could do it without at least knowing the professional helpers were just down the hall and would come running if I fell or couldn't manage things on my own.

Finally, on October 6, I was discharged from Magee. I was in physical therapy when my brother Jimmy came to pick me up. He had the biggest smile on his face. "Are you ready to go?" he asked.

I nodded. He waited patiently for me to finish therapy, then came into the room to help me gather my things. Just as I had vowed on the day I arrived, I planned to walk out of that hospital. Jimmy was there to help me do this.

Sonia had huge tears in her eyes as I lifted myself out of my wheelchair, and with the use of leg braces and a walker, I began to step out of the therapy room. The room erupted in thunderous applause from the other patients and therapists. I felt as though I had won a marathon.

I would miss all my friends at Magee. I remember a young mother named Susan who had wheeled over to me earlier that morning. Susan had a tumor removed from her spine, and doctors said she would never walk again. She was a deeply religious young woman with two of the cutest and best-behaved children a parent could ever ask for. Susan had entered Magee as I was regaining use of my legs. I had continually encouraged her, as well as everybody else there, to keep hope alive, to never give up. During that last morning, Susan leaned over to me with tears in her eyes, and she whispered congratulations in my ear. I felt so bad leaving her but said, "I know you will walk again one day." Susan leaned back in her chair with a gentle smile that said she hoped so, too.

As I stood outside the therapy room, I said my final good-byes and wished them all success in their own recovery. I couldn't help but tell them they could do the same if there was even the slightest hint of a possibility. "If I can throw away the wheelchair and walk, so can you. It takes a lot of work, but in the end it will pay off."

With one final wave, my brother Jimmy and I disappeared moments later behind the doors of the elevator.

It was a slow walk out the entrance of Magee with Jimmy rushing ahead to put things down and open the hospital door. He then assisted me with getting into the car and took the walker and my bag to the trunk.

I had accomplished what I set out to do. But there was more to do than I thought. The recovery was still far from over. My new life would focus on again finding "normal"—which would change every day until I was back to my old life. I wondered if I would ever get everything back or what my life would look like once my body had fully recovered.

Maybe, I thought, *I'll wake up from this horrible, horrible dream and find my place again. A place where I could depend on who I was and how I fit into this world that no longer made sense.*

Chapter 3

Finding My Way at Home

I FELT A CERTAIN LEVEL OF SADNESS AS WE pulled away from the curb outside Magee. I looked out to see the rehab hospital one last time. I felt happy that I wouldn't have to stay there any longer but was filled with a sadness that I was going to have to regain control of my real-world experience. My thoughts raced as I watched the life I had known fade as quickly as the sight of Magee in my side mirror.

My brother Jimmy was excited and chattered about things at home and how they had set my place up to make it easier for me to get around. It wasn't going to be like one of those day passes. I was going to have to be alone a lot, so they wanted to make sure I could handle things by myself. My mind quickly turned again to the future, and I began to get excited about returning home. It was a relief that they had thought to rearrange things for me. I wasn't quite sure what my challenges would be, but if they could think of at least some of them it would make my life a lot easier until I got better at getting around.

Leaving the hospital and going home was something I had dreamt about since the day I was injured. Wherever I'd been in my life before the construction accident, I had always looked forward to going home. I would see myself walking in the door, setting my keys on the table, grabbing a beer out of the refrigerator, taking a deep breath, and sinking into my favorite chair. My home was my sanctuary. When events played out in this scenario, I knew I was where I felt safe at the end of a long, trying day. I'd always be able to prepare for the onslaught of obstacles potentially presenting themselves the next day.

As Jimmy and I headed to my house, I felt ready to relax and re-energize in a similar way. I thought at least I would be in a position to control my environment once again by coming home and that it would assist in the healing process somehow. It was a great feeling to be going home for good.

Being able to overcome the devastating physical injuries gave me a feeling of invincibility. My will was as strong as ever. However, I had been so busy being the guy whose life got better every day that I forgot what it took to get there.

I hope never to forget the feeling of this moment, I thought. *Though I still have a very long road to travel in getting my life back, I have come an incredible distance. I now know I have what it took to travel that road.*

A Rough Start

The first few weeks at home were the scariest. Since I had the use of a walker to get around, we planned that I would be staying by myself. Magee had provided a wheelchair, but I couldn't maneuver it in my home as I felt necessary. Besides, I swore I would never get back in that chair. So many times it would have been much easier to cheat and use it for a just while, at least until I felt stronger. It was an exhausting effort to re-acclimate to my old surroundings.

Nights were the worst. What if I fell? Nobody would know. Then during the day, I constantly had to depend on others to assist me. Going out to buy groceries or getting to doctor appointments required the assistance of others. And if I were in the company of others, I would not have the fear of being left alone.

Besides adjusting to living back at home, I also had to get control of my construction business. My employees did a great job while I was in the hospital, but there was no one there to watch over things as I had. At least being out of the hospital, I could have someone drive me to a construction site to see first-hand what progress had been made. It gave me the opportunity to interact with *I was back in the real world working with real people and real situations that didn't allow for personal issues.* workers on the site to let them know I was back. During my time in the hospital, I was totally at the mercy of my brothers overseeing day-to-day situations. Even though we would discuss issues during visiting hours or over the phone, my need to control every facet of my life was put to the test. I had to let go, to a certain extent, and trust things would get done the way I would want them to get done. And for the most part they were. But they were handling what was currently happening while no one was out looking for future business opportunities. By this time, the economy had begun to slow down and less work was available.

My two brothers who worked for me were tremendous. I know it was difficult for them to pick me up each day and take me out for a few hours to check on the progress, schedules, and general day-to-day concerns. A few hours a day were all I could handle. I wore out easily and seemed to be tired all the time.

This wasn't like being in the hospital. I was back in the real world working with real people and real situations that didn't allow for personal issues. There were no allowances where business was concerned. The work was either done right, on time, and within budget or it wasn't. No excuses were acceptable—not even mine. Without my brothers, I would have probably lost it all. They helped save my business and my livelihood. Now it was time for me to get back into my old world, even if I could only visit it for a few hours a day.

Making Adjustments

Initially I had to travel to Magee three times a week to continue physical therapy; mainly this was because my legs were so weak. My stamina was virtually nonexistent. Life was not as I had planned it. It wasn't as I envisioned it, how I wanted it, or as I could accept it. I knew the work we were doing at Magee was my only hope for getting my life back. As much as I hated to return for therapy, I discovered a dependence on them for reaching a higher level of strength in my body and my mind. Sometimes they had more faith in my progress and the effects of my determination than I did. I felt both battered and renewed as the weeks passed.

At home, it was hard enough navigating to the bathroom or the bedroom, let alone trying to cook a meal or attempting to do laundry. Besides, at the pace I could move, everything seemed to be in super-slow time. Just getting dressed, or at least what I considered to be dressed at the time, was a 30-minute fiasco. Trying to clean up in the kitchen after a meal required a break halfway through. It was horrible. As much as I had detested being stuck behind the walls of Magee, I was beginning to develop a fondness for my time there. I'm not sure if this was because I was afraid of something or if I longed for some limited level of personal responsibility for a while longer.

Amanda came over as much as she could; she was an enormous help. I couldn't do much and I felt helpless. She helped clean, did laundry, and handled pretty much everything else that I started but couldn't finish. I think I was kidding myself that I could handle things.

Even going out was a hassle. For two months after my discharge, I needed a walker to get around. The number of people who stared at me as I attempted to maneuver through a restaurant was incredible. I wanted to shout, *Yes, I'm only thirty-one and using a walker. Can you just eat your dinner and leave me alone?* It wasn't their fault. It was my issue, and all the attention got to me. I reached a point where I didn't wish to go out in public at all. I wanted to stay at home and be miserable all by myself.

After the first few weeks, Amanda told me to come and stay with her until I was strong enough. That way, she could keep an eye on me and also wouldn't have to travel as much between her place and mine. I felt our relationship was progressing and decided it would be the best option for me. I must admit, I knew it would be nice to be around her more. It also meant I would have to work harder so she wouldn't think I was hopeless.

A Downturn Begins

As December was ending, I had been out of the hospital for almost three months, and I was becoming terribly miserable. My physical limitations were extraordinary. I had been one of the most independent people I'd ever known, and now I could do virtually nothing. I tired easily, couldn't drive myself anywhere, and felt very depressed about my situation.

Prior to my discharge, the doctor said I needed to be careful as winter approached and not to go out when it was snow-ing for fear of falling. Thanksgiving saw 4 inches of snow. I had never seen it snow that early in New Jersey. On the other hand, winter brought some advantages. I was always bundled up because I was cold, so no one could see the fiberglass shell I constantly wore to protect my back or the plastic leg braces that supported my walking.

There was one bright spot in the midst of my misery. I was able to discard the walker I had become so dependent upon. I had to be very careful, however, in making sure one foot stepped in front of the other at all times. But this was still progress.

I continued to improve, but not as quickly as I wanted. It never felt quick enough. I still didn't feel like a whole person because I remained so dependent upon others for help. By now, I had begun to withdraw from the world. I spent as much time alone as I could. It felt safe in the world I created in my head. I noticed this as my depression got deeper and deeper.

Even though I continued living at Amanda's and our relationship progressed, I spent much of the day alone with my thoughts. If I had to be somewhere, Amanda would take me if she was around or one of my brothers would come from a jobsite to pick me up. As soon as I got done with whatever it was, I wanted to be whisked back to Amanda's so I could hide out all by myself.

By spring, my legs had gotten strong enough to eliminate the braces. I was also able to get my driver's license back. Now I felt that I could regain more of my independence. Even so, the depression continued to deepen. I didn't care about anything. I started giving the minimal effort to everything—just enough to get by. Of course, all aspects of my life began to suffer—my relationships, my business, etc.

Problems Worsen

In July 1990, I returned to the orthopedic surgeon at Cooper Trauma Hospital for a one-year checkup. Everything seemed to be okay, so I was officially cleared to go back to work, although I had returned much earlier. The economy worsened. Though I was extremely limited in how much I could do, I did as much as possible to save my business. It was strictly supervision and administrative work. I was back on jobsites on a daily basis, but only as long as my stamina could hold up. Now it seemed as if the psychological aspects of being injured were having a more detrimental effect than the physical limitations.

At this time, I began to experience problems with my surgically repaired leg. The plate and screws used to reattach the leg caused pain every time I took a step. I returned to Cooper to have all that hardware removed. With my left leg again in a cast for six weeks, I was told not to work. How could I not work? My business had suffered so much over the past year because of the accident that I felt I might lose it altogether if I took more time off. I needed my business and it needed me.

By now, the depression had really begun to sink in and I couldn't shake it. I had spiraled too deep. This is not at all like me. I had always been so strong-willed and determined that if I put my mind to anything, anything at all, I could accomplish it.

By the time the leg cast came off, I had become a virtual recluse. I rarely went to the jobsites, stayed only long enough in the office to get major needs addressed, and hid out at Amanda's the rest of the time. Amanda was the person who could most easily see how I was continuing to slip into myself, as she was one of the very few people I had contact with. I would ask her to take messages when people called. If someone stopped by to see how I was doing, she would have to answer the door and tell them I wasn't feeling up to seeing visitors.

I wasn't sure I would ever be back to "normal." Was it worth everything I was going through?

When I drove around, I'd envision myself crossing into oncoming traffic and ending this perpetual misery once and for all. I didn't want to continue living any longer. I felt that my life absolutely sucked. I had beaten incredible odds overcoming catastrophic injuries, but I wasn't sure it was enough—at least at that moment. It was taking too long to get my life in order. I wasn't sure I would ever be back to "normal." Was it worth everything I was going through? While I felt as if I had won some sort of second-chance-at-life lottery—and I was very grateful for that—I felt that getting back to "normal" should be easier.

I wanted my old self to be there already—someone who could look back at me from the mirror with the same smile and the same knowledge that the world is a safe and beautiful place. Where was that person? I didn't remember much about him these days. I had lost that man and I couldn't figure out who stood in his place.

My recovery was too fast to get an idea of who I now was, yet too slow to see who I would become. The man standing in my shoes was living in a cocoon waiting to be reborn. *I am here now. I have had a defining moment that could have stopped my life.* The reality of this had smacked me in the face.

Construction was slowing down noticeably. My options were limited. Even if I gave up the dream of running my own show, larger companies were downsizing. It would be virtually impossible to find work with someone else.

Healing the Mind

After listening to family and friends suggest, cajole, harp, and bitch about my depression, my situation, my general attitude, and how I should be feeling grateful for everything in my life, I finally agreed to seek professional help. I had never done that before in my life. I was taught that you deal with your own problems and move on. Getting help was something very foreign to me, but I knew I had to make a conscious change to quit being a victim.

The diagnosis was Post-Traumatic Stress Disorder (PTSD). It is an anxiety disorder that often develops after exposure to a terrifying event in which grave physical harm occurred or was threatened. More and more, I was becoming emotionally numb to people around me as well as life in general. Flashbacks were constant, as if I were reliving the accident in my mind almost every day. I was easily startled in situations, especially in business, and I lost the ability to trust in myself. If you can't trust yourself, it's extremely hard to function. I know it was for me.

Nothing brought me joy. Each morning when I woke up, I longed for the night so I could go to bed and forget about the day.

Nothing brought me joy. Each morning when I woke up, I longed for the night so I could go to bed and forget about the day. That was something I had learned to do in the hospital purely for self-preservation. Sadly, I felt this way in the morning even though I had the potential of the day ahead of me. I often felt the progress was happening so slowly that I really didn't want to know the potential; it was most likely out of my reach and just another instance where I would be disappointed and frustrated.

I recall an incident that occurred soon after I arrived home. I discovered the bizarre effects the sound of a helicopter had on me. I was on the porch when I heard it. Suddenly I was paralyzed with fear. My body tensed and I closed my eyes. As the helicopter approached, I suddenly began to relive the accident: *The crash, the pain, the rescuers, and all the paralyzing fear that went along with it came back to me. All the while, everyone was scrambling around trying to save my life. I heard the sound of a helicopter moving closer and closer until the sound was virtually deafening. I was told that the helicopter was for me. No one knew I was afraid of flying. What if it crashed? I suppose at that point it didn't really matter. How much worse could it get? I didn't have much time left. I needed immediate critical medical care.*

As quickly as it came over me, the feeling subsided. I was back on my porch safe from the past. The helicopter wasn't for me this time. I had to sit down and process in my mind exactly what had just happened. I wondered if such reactions would ever go away. *Will I always find myself back in the midst of the accident when a helicopter flies by?*

Fortunately, the appointments with the psychiatrist were going well. It felt good to process what was happening to me. Not much in the long year made sense. I had so much to be grateful for, as everyone told me, but I also had so much to be angry about, which no one had to explain. As we sorted out the dichotomy, I realized that feeling both angry and grateful was a natural part of the process.

The psychiatrist and I talked for a while about helicopters and my experience on the porch. I thought only guys who came back from Vietnam had flashbacks like that. The time I spent getting to the hospital fell so short of a war experience, so why would I react as if I had gone through it? The doctor explained the possible causes and why the reaction occurred. I was put on a short-term medication. After a few visits, I began feeling better, and shortly thereafter, I was discharged from his care.

I realized, though, that this was the turning point to enter into a new life. I became aware for the first time that I couldn't deal with everything on my own. *There must be someone or something greater than me who oversees everything,* I thought. *There is way too much for me to control. I'm more than ready to hand the controls to someone else.* I felt at peace with this realization.

I had struggled so hard and so long, I'd exhausted myself. I discovered that as hard as I had worked and as much as I'd always been in control over the past year, I hadn't been in control of anything for very long. What had happened to me and how my body reacted did not come from me. Certainly I did what I was told, but at no time did I have control. I merely played out the actions that would help me accomplish my goal.

If I wasn't in control, where was it all coming from? What master plan was at work in my life? Had the accident been a part of it? Or was it just a random situation that can strike anyone at any time and I just happened to be the man standing in the wrong place? I couldn't ask *what if,* I could not think *why,* I could only realize that I am not in control and trust the power that was guiding me back toward the life I used to know or onward to something better.

Moving Forward Again

Less than two years after the accident, although it seemed like about 20, I started a new home-building business with three acquaintances. I knew I couldn't continue on my own. Then, within six years of being hurt, the financial losses I incurred were all recouped, and I was back again to the life I was comfortable living.

My thoughts, however, were focusing more and more on important issues rather than the kind of car in my driveway.

Funny how a life-threatening injury can make you stop to think about your purpose in life. What was mine? *Why are we here?* I wondered. *Why was I ever here? What is our purpose? Do I have a purpose? Have I accomplished this purpose? What is the meaning of life anyway?*

I have watched people growing up, growing old, being born, and dying, and yet I didn't really know what their purpose is or was. Do some people live and die without ever having a purpose? Or do they just say, "The heck with it. I want to live my life for the sole purpose of being happy in my own little world"? Do others think they can never accomplish anything great enough to be considered a purpose? Can you merely affect one person's life and consider that your entire life's purpose was accomplished? I didn't know the rules on that one. They were all important questions.

Why was I here? Why was my life spared? What purpose did I need to fulfill and when would it start? I needed to know. I wanted to know. I wanted it to be worth what I had gone through. I wanted it to begin after handling so much pain.

Time does heal all wounds, whether we want it to or not. It had been a long time since the accident, and I was not the person I was earlier. As I got to know who I had become, I couldn't imagine what used to be "me." My progress has not been linear; there have been many ups and downs. However, the change within has been exponential.

A New Kind of Life

Many people who have been through near-death or traumatic experiences believe that in some way they were blessed. I know my accident was a blessing. It took me quite a long time to find the blessing in it. Sure, merely surviving it was a blessing. The blessing of the accident, however, goes way beyond that.

My eyes were opened to another way of looking at life—a way I would never have seen had my life continued on without my whole world crashing down on top of me. Perhaps karma has allowed me a second chance to live. I could have gotten back into the old habits I lived by prior to being hurt. I did, in fact, in the years right after the accident. But there was something within that called for me to seek a different way, to seek my truth.

There was something within that called for me to seek a different way, to seek my truth.

As I sought that truth, I continued to be transformed. It took a long time to see the blessing, and I can't say that I have enjoyed any part of what happened to me. What I can say about the blessing is that I found a strength I would have never known I had. I am not an extraordinary man. I am a man who had a choice and drew strength from places I didn't know existed.

I found love all around me—love I had taken for granted and, quite frankly, didn't believe existed. The family I had cared so much for, and had loved only as I knew to love before the accident, were people who have given love back to me in ways I would never have expected.

Though I had always respected my body, I never appreciated how intricate it is. Something as small as bundles of nerves can, when injured, cause devastating changes to one's body. Or how the motor pathway from the brain controls every function in the human body and, when this flow is interrupted, can change the course of one's life. Conversely, even when extreme trauma is inflicted upon the body, miraculous recoveries are possible, and they do happen every day. Maybe not to the extent of what I experienced, but miraculous nonetheless.

I've found that I have grown. Life is now much deeper, richer, and more fulfilling than I could ever have imagined. I can no longer feel the same about *anything*. I only know there is a better way to live, and if I can grow so much over a short amount of time, there has to be more that I can achieve. It won't take a building to fall on me again to open my eyes. I don't have all the answers, by any means, but I have had the questions—and the motivation to see where this revelation will take me.

PART II
WHAT I'VE
LEARNED SINCE

"Faith is not the knowledge
of what the mystery of the Universe is,
but the conviction that there is a mystery,
and that it is greater than us."

~ Rabbi David Wolpe

Chapter 4

My Spiritual Journey

IF YOU HAD ASKED ME 20 YEARS AGO WHAT spiritual evolvement was, I would have scratched my head. Remember, I'm a guy who tried to make a deal with God at the lowest point in his life. *Let me walk again and I will go back to church. Please!* My spiritual development began when I died but then came back to life at the accident site, and it has become an incredible adventure.

One of the reasons I put off writing this book was that what I've learned never ends. Once you choose to get on this ride of discovery, it becomes far too difficult to get off. You cannot unlearn what you know. It seeps down deep. It grows deeper, too, the farther you choose to journey. It is like deciding to walk through a door only to find the room filled with other doors staring you in the face. You get to choose which door you will pass through, although sometimes that decision is easier said than done.

As I journey along this path, I am amazed to meet people who have had teachers show them the way. They were the obedient students, able to hear what they needed and apply it to their lives in a very practical way. My path was, and continues to be, different. I cannot quite figure out why, but it really doesn't matter. You might say I have learned a little from a lot of masters (and some not so masterful) along the way. Perhaps that's the way the Universe, or God, would have me search it out. I've always listened to the opinions of others but ultimately made my own decisions.

Growing Up Catholic

Every association I had with the church was negative. I couldn't see how this would be a benefit to me.

My early childhood was spent in a constant state of fear. I never felt safe at home because of my father's alcoholism and the overall family dysfunction. Plus my mother's fear of life was absorbed by her children. By the time God was introduced, I was ready for some help. But the God I heard about wasn't what I had hoped for. I was raised in the Catholic faith. My earliest memory of church was being forced to go to Sunday school as a little boy. One Sunday, I was taught that I was going to die one day. I never knew that. I didn't even understand what death was. From that moment on, everything related to God became fearful. If we weren't good, God was going to punish us. If we didn't do what we were told, God would impose some unspeakable tragedy in our lives. I couldn't imagine living my entire life in fear of Him. Everything about the church was always predicated with an element of fear—at least that's how I perceived it.

My mother used God to get us boys to behave. *God is watching you.* More fear. Also, in my early childhood years, many of my older relatives died and I had to attend funeral masses. I automatically associated church with sad occasions. It seemed that, as a young child, every time I entered a church people were crying. It never was an uplifting experience for me.

Every association I had with the church was negative. I couldn't see how this would be a benefit to me. Even though I know the exact opposite is true today, there are times when entering a church will bring back those sad early childhood memories.

I still recall the day before my First Communion when I stood in line at the church with other children waiting to give my initial confession to a priest. I felt tremendous anxiety as I anticipated going behind the closed door of the confessional. I didn't have a clue what I was going to say as I stood in line with my classmates. As the line continued to move me closer to the confessional, I could feel my heart pounding louder and louder. I worried about confessing things that might make me come across as a bad kid. Then again, I was afraid that if I didn't tell everything, God would know I wasn't being totally truthful and I'd receive even more punishment.

The final straw, for me, was attending catechism as a 13-year-old. My mother forced us to go because one of my brothers and I disrespected a priest, at least in her opinion. One night in class, a friend of mine started joking around and got the entire class giggling. Obviously, this did not sit well with the nun. All the kids could not stop laughing. The more we laughed, the madder the nun got. As her level of anger increased, it served to ratchet up the volume of laughter from the students. Finally, at her ultimate point of frustration, the nun screamed out that we would all burn in hell for what we were doing.

I remember walking home that night with my brother thinking, *I've had it! I refuse to continue this farce of living my life in fear of a god sitting on a cloud watching and waiting for me to make a mistake just so he could hurt me.* Besides, I had too many other things from my upbringing to be fearful of. The constant screaming matches between my parents, my father's angry outbursts after too much alcohol, my mother's fear of having to deal with reality. I quit going to church on a regular basis and decided I would rely on myself. That way, I could avoid getting hurt. It would also relieve some of the everyday fear that I couldn't shake. I thought perhaps if I led a good life, I wouldn't be judged unkindly by God. Mainly, I felt that my own inner sense of right and wrong could guide me. This new approach worked well, and it allowed me to have some of the peace that I had been missing for such a long time.

During my early adult years, I had a lot of questions about God as the result of my Catholic upbringing. For instance, if God did exist, how could He be so judgmental? After all, we were created in his image (according to what I had been taught). If God was perfect and it was a sin when we got angry, how come God could be angry with us most of the time and it wasn't a sin?

How could we continuously be judged? Were good deeds ever counted? Or was it that we had to remember all of our sins and make sure we confessed them to get absolved because absolution was the key? Were good deeds just a bonus in case there was a tie in the end and God was wavering about letting someone into Heaven? Who was the priest anyway, and why did we have to confess to him? Why did I have to talk to the priest instead of talking to God himself? Wasn't I good enough for God to talk to? If God wouldn't communicate with me and I needed a priest, maybe I could just slip under the radar and not be noticed at all.

Testing the Spiritual Waters

It seems that the white-light moment I experienced during the accident activated a switch inside of me. After that critical point, I was set to embark on the long, arduous quest to find the meaning of life, at least in my experience. This near-death experience was so beautiful. I felt warmth. I no longer hurt. I felt at peace, and although I didn't know what would happen next, I recall feeling absolutely no fear at that moment. I knew everything was okay.

A "near-death experience" has been defined as a varying range of experiences associated with impending death or doom. Experiences have included detachment from the body; total serenity; feelings of levitation, security, and warmth; as well as the presence of a bright light. Some people experienced a bright pointed light as if they were in a tunnel. Others, including myself, experienced the feeling of being enveloped totally in a bright white light. Some have interpreted the light phenomenon as God or some spiritual presence. Science has learned over the past three decades that people who have these experiences report an effect on their motivations, values, and conduct. These people tend to fear death less than they may have before, they begin to live their lives more fully, and they discover a stronger sense of purpose.

Bartering with God has a whole new flavor to it when your life is on the line.

A few weeks after the accident, when I was medically stable, my friends joked with me: "What did you do to deserve this?" Though I thought about it, I couldn't answer that question. I'll admit, I have done some things in my life that I'm not proud of, but never, ever would I have done something so despicable to deserve what happened to me. I now know to file this experience under "stuff happens."

Bartering with God has a whole new flavor to it when your life is on the line. It's not quite the same as when you want the new girl at work to like you or want a new car when you can't quite conceive how you're going to pay for it. This was my offer: *Allow me to walk again and I'll go back to church.* I had questioned His existence for the previous 15 years, and yet I was asking to be made whole again. Actually, I was in a place where the only viable thing to do was pray.

Inside, I clung to the belief that God did exist and He was the only option, the only hope, I had. Nothing of the world I had lived in could help me through this. I wanted God to be real for the first time in my life, and I knew that if He were real, I had a chance to walk again. It might take some bargaining, but it was the only chance I had. The most powerful thing about the entire experience was to hear that voice speak to me. It spoke with a calm, precise, and to-the-point attitude, not a bellowing, booming voice judging what I had done or pointing to my disbelief in Him. No one else was in the room; I was alone. I really felt unconditional love for the very first time.

From the moment God spoke to me in the hospital, telling me, Bill Shaner specifically, that I would be okay, that I would recover, that I would walk again, I knew I had a spiritual partner. As I mentioned, this moment was the first time I had experienced unconditional love. The more I am aware of the unconditional love that God provides, the more inner intuitiveness appears in my life experience.

After the accident, my motivations did change. What was important prior to it was no longer a priority afterwards. This was not an immediate shift in perspective, but rather a gradual intuitive feeling that has become more pronounced over the years.

In the years since the accident, I have become a person of refined kindness and compassion, providing as much unconditional love as I can possibly give. Three of my major values prior to the accident were money, competition, and power. Although money is required in order to subsist, the three do not have their hold on me at the same level as before. I have learned that humans become more successful when creating through cooperation rather than competition. My life has evolved into one of acceptance of others as they are. As a result, my tendency to be judgmental has dissipated over time. My life has shifted from selfish concerns to a desire to help others succeed.

Uncovering Blessings

My accident was a blessing. Not the physical pain I endured and continue to endure from time to time, but the experience itself. It launched an inner journey to seek answers—answers about me, about life, who I am, and why am I here. Since the day of the accident, I've had many opportunities to experience spirituality. As I said, it has been an incredible journey. Make your own decision; decide which door you'll open next. If you want your life to get better, you'll need to grow, and you must choose to go to the next level.

Many of us try to ride just under the radar. I did it for years. We might hope God will not find us and that we'll never have to do more than scratch the surface. Some folks actually believe that attending church on Sunday for an hour or so protects them so they have the rest of the week to be and do whatever they want; they've been forgiven. Then, next week, it's back to church to get forgiven again without ever changing anything. No evolving, just repenting to keep on the path to Heaven.

Have the churches failed us in this way? Have they made us feel that it's all about being forgiven for things we have no intention to stop doing? This was not enough for me. I was either going to stay away or take the journey. And I had promised God that I'd return to church if he helped me walk again.

Spirituality as Motivation

As I look back over my life, I realize that I have passed through many doors. Although not always consciously aware of it, at times I have yearned to find the true essence of life—*what it's all about.* In my early adult years, when I was taking care of myself from a spiritual standpoint, I studied everything I could get my hands on as it related to motivation and the study of human potential. This included the ideas of Tony Robbins, Wayne Dyer, Stephen Covey, Jim Rohn, Zig Ziglar, W. Clement Stone, and others. In spite of my upbringing, I was always an optimistic and self-motivated individual. This material reinforced that feeling, but that's all it was: just a feeling with no depth to it.

Yes, motivation is very important, and I use it all the time to help people get unstuck from their present situations. Motivational techniques can provide a person with the opportunity to see a situation differently when what appears to be hopeless is actually far from it. Stories of the human spirit—by this, I mean having perseverance and faith in your inner strength—are uplifting and can inspire. For instance, Henry Ford went bankrupt five times before he started a company that some of you send your payments to every month. A strong human spirit and a deep self-belief, along with determination, prevail.

The same is true of Colonel Sanders. He operated a small but successful restaurant in Corbin, Kentucky. When the interstate system was being constructed in this country in the 1950s, Sanders realized it would have a grave impact on his business. So in 1955, at the age of 65, the Colonel hit the road in his old Cadillac with a monthly pension of $105 and his trusty chicken recipe. He traveled from restaurant to restaurant trying to sell his approach to cooking chicken.

According to the story, he was told "no" 1,008 times before he made his first sale. Yet he continued, sometimes sleeping in his car to save money. Restaurateur number 1,009 gave him his first "yes." After two years of daily sales calls, the Colonel had signed up a total of five restaurants that bought his chicken recipe. The Colonel, however, continued to believe in himself and his product. He pressed on, knowing that one day his idea would pay off—and it did. By 1963, the Colonel had six hundred restaurants selling his chicken. And in 1964, he was bought out for a price of $2 million.

And what about Ray Kroc? He was a restaurant equipment salesman who sold milkshake machines to the McDonald brothers in Southern California in the 1950s. Kroc had a vision, he partnered with the brothers, and eventually this businessman bought them out. The rest, they say, is history. According to McDonald's February 2009 annual sales report, their restaurants bring in 8.1 percent of all restaurant sales in the United States today. And see how far you travel next time you leave the house before you see the golden arches. My point is that motivation is important, but if you don't have a connection deep within, it's nothing more than a temporary warm and fuzzy feeling.

Motivation is important, but if you don't have a connection deep within, it's nothing more than a temporary warm and fuzzy feeling.

A Better Approach

For many years, my god was the almighty dollar. Meanwhile, major inner issues festered below the surface. I had a huge axe to grind with life for what I thought was an unfairly harsh childhood, and I was determined to make up for it and get even. This motivation was just window-dressing that lacked substance; I continuously remained unfulfilled. It didn't matter what relationship I was in, what car I bought, or where I lived. No matter what it was, it never satisfied me. My life was a continuous merry-go-round of working to obtain something, obtaining it, and then realizing it wasn't fulfilling.

The accident provided me an opportunity, albeit a rather painful one, to stop and catch my breath. As I recovered, I slowly realized that I had come to a fork in the road. I had to choose which way to travel. For several years, I decided to try to traverse two roads at the same time. While utilizing the motivational forces to heal my physical injuries, on the inside I was trying to resolve the issue of my experience with God.

I had promised to go back to church if I had the opportunity to walk again. I did walk again. Maybe there was something more to life, if I chose to explore below the surface. The accident and its aftermath could not be some freak random experience in life. Did stuff like this just happen? Did stuff like this happen for a reason? If it did, then why? I knew simply existing was not going to answer these questions. I also knew that simply existing was not enough—*not anymore.* Maybe life does give us signs, only it is up to us to choose whether to listen.

Six years after the accident, I finally gave in and returned to church. My part of the bargain had at last been upheld. I needed to try to find answers to my questions. In the years immediately after the accident, I had allowed fear to consume me. I had tremendous physical difficulties to overcome. Tremendous financial difficulties also ensued. I worked as hard as humanly possible and I did overcome it all. Outwardly, no signs existed any longer of the devastating experience I had gone through a mere six years earlier. All my debts had been cleaned up in the aftermath of the accident, and I'd just finished building a new home.

On the surface, I was back to my old self. But as I sat in front of a roaring fire in my new house, I looked around and realized that this didn't do it for me either. Some deep, large black hole within me screamed out for answers. I couldn't ignore that hole anymore. That night I decided to start looking for those answers.

Growing up, I knew only that Catholicism was not working for me. I am not judging it, merely giving my opinion. God on a cloud that only the priests could talk to, an angry God punishing everyone for their sins, and having to confess to the priest—not to mention the little irritations of my particular church—it all made me want to run and hide.

I remember the parish my family belonged to had a very long but narrow parking lot immediately adjacent to the church. Every Sunday, men guided parishioners entering the lot into long back-to-front lines of parked cars. After mass ended, people exited the church and, if the drivers in front of them did not return as quickly to their cars, they'd be stuck in their car until the other churchgoers returned. Many Sundays, car horns were blowing in that lot and people yelled angrily for others to hurry up and move their cars. To me, that is not what Sunday and worshiping God was supposed to be about. Such memories of my childhood had kept me away from churches.

I decided, after much trepidation, to try an interdenominational church service. I figured it wouldn't stray too much from what I was accustomed to, and if there really were a fearful, vengeful God, I would not burn in hell for going. In one of my experiences at this church, a pastor told the story of how he was working on Wall Street, 100 pounds over weight, having a difficult time in his marriage, feeling despondent, and on the verge of giving up. He went to a church service, found God (I didn't know He could be missing!), and within one week was on a street corner in New York City with a Bible in his hand preaching the Word. The man standing before me was an inspired, fit, healthy man who seemed to have it together.

I was hoping for an epiphany myself, but not necessarily like that. It was in that timeframe, though, that I began to find answers. The sermon I had heard inspired me and made me believe that there was more to know. I could walk again, but I still felt something must be missing. I wondered whether God might be able to answer some of the questions I had about spirituality in general and about other areas of my life which were not exactly as I wanted them.

A Spiritual Awakening

When I quietly contemplated the existence of God, answers appeared. Thus began my own re-birth of faith in a way that completely related to me. I cannot tell you how many times I sat in church on Sunday baffled that the pastor's message was meant specifically for me—directed to whatever problem I was trying to work out. At times, I just wanted to say, "Thank you, God, for bringing all these people out to hear what you had to tell me!" I suppose you might call it a sort of quiet epiphany.

The church I attended was a newly built structure that could fit 1,200 people, and usually both Sunday services were packed. The pastor was an extremely engaging and charismatic personality. As I reflect on that time, I believe the Universe was using others to prove God's existence to me. I know it was because I had not allowed myself to get quiet and go within, to trust the still small voice within me. I had no prior experiences with that.

Here I had just begun to contemplate the existence of God, and I went to one of these church services, only to have the pastor start out with "You know, I come across many people who ask how do I know that God truly exists?" He certainly had my attention, as that was the predominant question I had had on my mind for weeks. The pastor concluded: "… and my answer simply is I know that I know that I know." At that exact moment, I welled up with an incredible inner feeling that I knew it all to be true. I knew within that this was the truth.

Enough with the negative "thou shalt not" experience! I knew what I should not do—I wanted guidance on where to go, what to do, and how to do it.

There are many other examples I could cite of being tuned in to God's guidance, from meeting a specific person at the right time to working on a problem and then listening to the radio and something speaking directly to me. Now this kind of coincidence occurs all the time in my life.

The only catch remaining in my mind was this sort of conditional aspect in organized religion—that you had to do certain things in order to be "saved." I found this disconcerting. I guess organized religion suits the lifestyles of many people, giving them purpose and hope, and in every way is exactly what they need. The bottom line is that each person needs to decide, after all, how they are going to travel their own spiritual journey. What is right for them is right for them.

In my heart, as "my religion" formed, I couldn't see nor grasp the fact that God was separate from us or that he sat in judgment of all. This did not resonate within me. I needed to find something with positive guidance to it. Enough with the negative "thou shalt not" experience! I knew what I *should not* do—I wanted guidance on where to go, what to do, and how to do it.

I don't consider myself a sinner anymore. I make mistakes like everyone else, but I take responsibility, learn from it, and do better the next time the situation arises. I am too busy trying to move forward to get stuck on the insignificant issues. This includes certain rules of the church which I do not agree with.

I kept returning to the night in the hospital when God spoke directly to me. I knew I was not crazy. There was no burning bush in the room, but I was sure of my experience. Pretty sure, I thought. If the experience didn't happen, then why did I walk again when doctors said I wouldn't? Why did I dwell on this voice that I heard in my head telling me that I would recover? Things unfolded the more I contemplated it, but they didn't happen fast enough. My next level of investigation was about to begin.

Seek and Ye Shall Find

In the spring of 2000, I moved to Florida. I'd had an inner calling about Florida since my college days but never followed it. I guess I wasn't listening. The moment I arrived there, I knew this was where I was supposed to be. I visited a friend who suggested I come down and check it out. Within two months of that visit, I had sold my interest in a homebuilding business in New Jersey, sold my house, bought a house, and found a job. It was almost too easy how things fell into place.

The Nirvana did not last too long, however. Within 18 months of my arrival, I had gotten divorced, lost all the money I had worked so hard to regain after my accident, and was left alone 1,200 miles from what I had always known as my life. Still, I had this overwhelming inner knowing that Florida was where I was supposed to be. I think sometimes life needs to strip us away from what we think we want in order to put us on the path of where we really want to go.

Somewhat depressed and unsure about everything at that point, I found a husband-and-wife team of therapists who were also pastoral counselors. The Reverends Sam and Bunny Sewell were not your typical pastoral counselors. A little older than me, these two people came across as friends upon our initial introduction. It was as if they stood waiting for my arrival in order to help me clear my head, take a breath, and begin moving forward with my life.

Initially I didn't even know they were pastoral counselors. The ad I saw described their practice as a counseling and training facility. During sessions with them, the spiritual realm I sought began to manifest. My first few visits centered on what I perceived my problems to be. They taught me about self-actualization, rational-emotive therapy, and my personality type so I might understand where I was and where I could go. It was during these visits that I began asking questions about religion and spirituality. Along with the program I was working on from a counseling perspective, they sprinkled in ideas from realms of theology.

It was incredible; each question brought answers that begged for more questions. My mind was opened to other philosophies and religions that seemed so foreign yet had some level of appeal to me. This all made a lot of sense and helped in answering questions about what had been going on in my life. They gave me the freedom to choose—to take what I wanted or needed from each concept we discussed and leave the rest.

Spirituality was no longer a religion. It was so much more—and it could be customized. The Reverends Sewell gave me books and recordings to review. The first recording I listened to really stuck with me. As I drove home the first night after our session, I popped a tape into the cassette player. The first words I heard were "When the student is ready, the teacher will appear." I knew then that the therapists were my teachers, and I was ready to become their student.

My hands tightened on the steering wheel as I braced myself. I imagined being jolted into the ride of my life. The hair raised on my arms and the back of my neck. This was the door, and I wanted to have it all in that split second. I spent three months with them and kept in touch for a few years afterward. That was the first opportunity I had to realize that there are many doors you can walk through. You merely need to be open to the opportunities so that when they present themselves, you are ready to allow them to unfold.

A Collaborative Effort

I am still in Florida and the spiritual growth has continued. Though it can happen and does happen every place on Earth, for me, Florida was key to finding my way spiritually. Perhaps I had to leave the familiar in order to transform without the influence of all the people who would lovingly encourage me to remain the man they knew. I *had* to change. I was a good man, yet the more I turned within and listened to that still small voice, the more answers I received. Maybe not all the answers I wished to hear, but all I needed to hear. There were still times of doubt, but they were of my own doing. I had to keep going. My life had changed; I needed to continue growing. I needed to keep opening the doors. Life *does* have a purpose. I couldn't return to being the person I used to be; that Bill died under the rubble years ago.

I have come to believe that we create our reality by our thoughts. I also believe, however, that inexplicable things happen to us through natural law. My life philosophy does differ with some who think we create our reality 100 percent. I think we all have random experiences as part of life. Tragedies of some sort happen to all of us. No one has a perfect life free of accidents, health problems, and upsets. It is how we respond to these events that shape our lives through our experiences.

Some might say, "If God truly exists, then why did He allow this (something like the accident) to happen?" I believe that when things like my accident happen (and they do happen in everyone's lives) that God is there to surround and protect you in many different ways. I say this because I have come to believe God is within us, not outside and separate from us. How could Jim and the others on the construction site that day find me buried under the rubble? Why, then, did expert medical care arrive when it did? How were they able to stabilize me so quickly, load me into a helicopter, and get me to the nearest trauma center as quickly as they did without causing me further injury? I could go on and on. Without the expertise and precision in the day's events, I would not have made it at all. It seemed to me to have been divinely orchestrated.

I have been blessed to experience the healing hand of the Universe (God). In the years since the accident, my faith has blossomed into a spiritual journey to seek out God in a deeper sense. Many, many times since this incident, I have seen God's hand at work. At first, this was very subtle, perhaps occurring by coincidence, but the signs are more plentiful and more apparent. They have probably existed throughout my life, but I am now more tuned in to noticing them.

During my journey, my vibratory level has become much more refined. I know others have not had the opportunity to witness what I have. But God doesn't need to open up the sky to show what His desire is for your life. I have learned that I don't need to go it alone anymore. I have my co-pilot. Together, we co-create. It is a collaborative effort. I know that if I am in proper alignment with God (the Universe), I can be what I *will* to be. And that is all I need to know.

Hebrews 11:1 (NRSV) says, *"Now faith is the assurance of things hoped for, the conviction of things not seen."* When I align my life with this knowledge, I remain anchored in the truth that God is the source. Faith is not conditional, nor is God's love. I learned this valuable lesson the day God spoke to me in the hospital. In time, I also learned to rely on faith, especially in those times when I operate in fear. I use faith to center myself, believing that my highest good will come from whatever situation unfolds before me.

In the first few years after the accident, I literally and figuratively got back on my feet. I tried to answer for myself what happened and, occasionally, why it happened. I worked at getting my business rolling again and at cleaning up the incredible debt that had piled up after the accident. Fear was a constant visitor. It is like a cancer; if allowed, fear will spread and destroy everything in its path. I can't claim that I was free from fear prior to and after the accident; I have operated from fear at times. But that fear is now countered with the personal experience I had with God back in the hospital.

I still had to figure out how to bring God forth at *all* times, though. As I tried to rely on Him more, I often went within to summon His help, only to follow up with, "It's okay now, God. I got it from here." Nothing could have been further from the truth! I laugh now thinking how egotistical it was to think I knew better than God (that divine spark within me) how to solve these problems. To think I was so desperate for an answer yet turned my back on the very part of me that could do the best job!

Clarifying Old Beliefs

The teachings of Jesus go beyond what I was taught as a child. For me, this was a revelation. I knew all the stories and thought I understood their meanings. When I finally returned to church, to keep up my end of the bargain, I also began reading the Bible. Based on what I had learned as a child, some things made sense; some did not. I developed an insatiable urge to study this book and turned within to ponder it. In the Bible, Jesus provides instructions to create the miracles necessary in our lives and the lives of those around us for complete fulfillment. *Who knew?*

Incredible! We have the ability to do the things Jesus was able to do—and even greater.

I believe we all have the power Jesus had within Him. John 14:12-14 (NRSV) says, "Very truly, I tell you, the one who believes in me (Jesus) will also do the works that I do and, in fact, will do greater works than these, because I am going to the Father. I will do whatever you ask me in my name, so that my Father may be glorified in the Son. If in my name you ask me for anything, I will do it."

Incredible! We have the ability to do the things Jesus was able to do—and even greater. I have used this belief to do some extraordinary things myself—not only at the time of my accident, but many times since. Jesus was truly the one who knew God was within, not separate and external, and this is what his ministry was all about. After the crucifixion, His disciples were to go out and teach "the way."

Now I'm not saying my way is the *only* way. We all have a choice about what to believe, whether we are spiritually minded or not. Also, we can choose not to believe and think the world is just a random series of unconnected events. But if you go within yourself to find greater meaning and purpose in life, I believe your life will be more fulfilling, with deeper meaning and purpose. I don't think anyone can say one religion (or path of spirituality) is the correct one. I also believe many people on the spiritual or religious path are more focused on "the aboutness," or talking the talk, rather than walking the walk.

Your spiritual path is *personal.* There are many ways; choose one and set a clear goal to find the answers *you* seek. When you receive an answer, ask another question. Ask for guidance—*a lot.* In addition, it's important to look behind the façade, or all the political and social teachings of your church (what it may stand for). Only then will you uncover the cornerstone—you'll find love. That's right, love is vital to the foundation of all spirituality. When you begin with love, you are on the right path.

When you begin with love, you are on the right path.

My favorite passage in the Bible is Luke 5:15 (NRSV): "*But now more than ever the word about Jesus spread abroad; many crowds would gather to hear him and be cured of their diseases.*" Some men brought a paralyzed man into town to be cured. Jesus had retreated into a home to teach. Because of the size of the crowd, the men had to climb onto the roof, tear an opening in it, and lower the man down before Him. Upon seeing their faith, Jesus cured the paralyzed man. Jesus said to the paralyzed individual (Luke 5:24), "*I say to you, stand up and take your bed and go to your home.*" In my personal experience, I have taken up my bed. My faith has healed me.

Few of us live up to our infinite possibility. I know I don't sometimes. We keep getting, or at least allowing ourselves to get, stuck in our old patterns of thought. When the newness of an idea begins to wane, we return to old safe patterns, no matter how difficult they may be. Instead, accept what the Universe has in store for you. You are a unique spiritual being, and you are on this planet for a purpose, should you decide to accept it. Of course, you can also continue to float through your misery of mediocrity. I hope not, but don't let someone else choose your path. You must learn to listen to your inner wisdom and embrace that vision for your life.

When things are going badly, it's easy to give up and throw in the towel. If you want to, then shame on you. Yes, the world is mad. Yes, bad news fills the papers and prevails on TV. Yes, there is bad news when you look over your shoulder. But I'm not joining the naysayers. I keep moving forward. When things are tough, it's certainly more difficult to look at the good. During these times, I continue to connect with people who are my friends. I continue to give out unconditional love. I continue to connect with my inner being. And you know what? It allows me to re-focus on the tasks at hand to move my life forward. It allows me, even if for only a moment, to catch my breath. It is my faith that allows me to continue to seek my life's desires. This reminds me of a poem by Patrick Overton that I came across many years ago.

Faith

When you walk to the edge of all the light you have
and take that first step into the darkness of the unknown,
you must believe that one of two things will happen:
There will be something solid for you to stand upon,
or, you will be taught to fly.

© Patrick Overton
The Leaning Tree, 1976
Rebuilding the Front Porch of America, 1997

In my greatest moment of the unknown, I had faith. Perhaps not to the level I thought I had, but it was true faith. I walked to the edge of all the light I had. I took that first step into the darkness of the unknown. I was taught to fly.

Chapter 5

Pouring a Solid Foundation (Basic Life Tenets)

ON SOME LEVEL, WE ALL WANT CHANGE. WE all want to be successful in life, whether it is in our careers, relationships, investments, or whatever might be important to us. Well, here's the good news: Success, joy, wealth, love, and fulfillment are all available right now! However, most of us don't have a path cleared for us. Whatever level of success we wish to achieve requires a willingness to overcome obstacles along the way. If we choose to take action and hit the obstacles head on, we can overcome them. If we choose to make excuses, success will be difficult to attain.

Even more importantly, our comfort zone plays a key role. We know what we have, and as bad as it may be, it's familiar. Change is unfamiliar, and it takes us out of that "safe" zone. There's always part of us that wants to do what we have always done and come up with different results regardless. Sometimes we do delve into a strategy to break the cycle. We may make headway toward our goals. Yet when fate causes struggles, we run and hide, moaning that it just wasn't meant to be. Meanwhile, you could be changing your direction in life so that it will lead you to success, love and joy, peace of mind, and contentment.

What makes the difference between a successful person and an unsuccessful person? Money? Family? Intellect? None of these. It's all about *you* and how you see yourself in this life experience. You're always going to be right. If you see yourself successful and happy, you will be. If you see yourself as a miserable loser, you will be. It is your choice—so see yourself as you want to be.

A Life Blueprint

We need to apply basic life tenets as we walk through our days headed toward a destination called "success." Many of our outside experiences are a direct result of how we see ourselves. It is much like raising a building. Blueprints provide a plan. They guide each step in the process. The finished product—what people see—is dependent on those plans. For each of us, what develops within is directly related to what we perceive on the outside. Inner and outer are connected. You become what you believe you are or can become.

Many of our outside experiences are a direct result of how we see ourselves. It is much like raising a building. Blueprints provide a plan.

Many of us have emotional addictions that keep us stuck in the same rut. I know from personal experience that many of my emotional addictions date back to my childhood. I am the person I am today because of them. I suppose, however, if we boiled down my issues they would be (or used to be) anger, resentment, and a victim mentality. Ultimately, everything is reduced to being a victim or a victor. As a victim, we aren't in control, which means nothing is our fault. Someone else caused our problems and we have to live with what they caused to happen in our lives.

On the next page is an exercise to help you understand what your chosen perception can do and how it can affect your judgment.

You have the power to change your perception and move forward. This is what it means to be the victor. I could mope around and blame others for my story. Instead, I chose to move forward, knowing that there really was no one to blame. That includes *me*—I am not to blame. I did not bring it upon myself. Life has ups and downs.

I have learned to incorporate many positive attitudes into my life. They have served me well in overcoming many situations I might have otherwise used to stifle the joys, loves, and successes that make me feel absolutely blessed. If I can do it, I know it is possible for everyone to do it. When these deep inner issues bubble up, the answer is to look at them, neutralize them using a different perspective, and trust it will do no good

The Eye of the Beholder

Read the following lines several times using different attitudes, such as joy, anger, or kindness and love. Finally, read the questions with no emotion, keeping your voice neutral.

- *What are you doing?*
- *Can I depend on you?*
- *Is that what you really think?*
- *How did you manage that?*

Notice the difference implied with each attitude. When these questions are stated with anger, they seem accusatory and degrading. Yet when these questions are repeated with a neutral tone, they are merely questions from someone who either just wants to know or is making polite conversation.

The perception changes when the attitude is kind and loving. The questions take on the power of encouragement and support from someone who may think you have the greatest ideas or methods and they want to understand them better.

My point? No matter what your situation, you can choose to perceive things differently.

to continue examining the situation. It doesn't serve anyone, especially you, to remain focused on something, particularly when you may have added a negative spin to it. Understand that it will not help you evolve into the person you were put on this earth to be. Focusing on the issue will get you stuck dwelling on the bad and not allow you to move through it and eventually past it.

We all have an inherent power that propels us, inspires us, and spurs us on to greater things. Science calls it the "unified field." Einstein theorized that everything emanates from a single source and returns to that same source. Theology calls it "God." Spirituality calls it "Universal Intelligence." Whatever you wish to call it … *it exists.* Everyone who works on personal growth eventually comes to the realization that a power greater than themselves can propel them to achieve their desires. To harness this power and get it to work with you, and not against you, you must realize it emanates from within and not from external sources.

Back in the late 1800s, a book titled *Acres of Diamonds* was published. It was written by Russell Cromwell, a preacher and storyteller.

The story Cromwell wrote still rings true today. It revolves around a Persian farmer who has much wealth but whose sole desire in life is to search for more. A visitor arrives at the farm and relates a story about finding diamonds and how the people who are finding these diamonds are becoming wealthy. The farmer wants so much to become wealthier that he decides he will go out and search for these diamonds. In order to begin this search, the farmer sells the farm and all his worldly possessions. He then heads out seeking his fortune. He searches and searches and searches but cannot find any diamonds. The farmer keeps on searching until he has spent his entire wealth looking in vain. Finally, destitute and out of options, the farmer throws himself into the sea.

Some years later, a man traveling through the area stops by the Persian's original farm. Upon entering the house, he sees a large, shiny object on the mantel of the fireplace. Admiring the beauty of the stone, he realizes that it is a huge diamond. He asks the keeper of the farm, "Where did this beautiful object come from?" The keeper motions toward the stream running behind the farm. It turns out the stone on the mantel was one of the world's largest diamonds and the farm sat atop one of the world's largest diamond mines. The moral of the story is that many times we look for solutions through external sources when they are within us waiting to be discovered.

We have vast resources at our disposal—more than we could comprehend. We have life experience to draw upon as well as the life experiences of others. I know that if I can overcome paralysis, I can overcome anything. You can, too, without having to ex- perience something so devastating. Many of us think we need external possessions to reach our fulfillment. Yet the power within gives us the ability to make choices that take us to what is truly fulfilling. The choices we make determine our future.

Many of us are a single idea away from being a success.

Many of us are a single idea away from being a success. Many of us may only need one or two numbers to uncover the combination of the lock. One idea could furnish the in- spiration needed to go to another level. A horse that garners 10 times the prize money of other horses is not 10 times faster but perhaps only a nose faster. In baseball, a good hit- ter hits .300. In reality, that is only three times in every 10 at-bats. But the good players, the ones who garner the huge contracts, make contact only a few more times than the aver- age player. You see, you don't need to be way out in front; you need only a little edge. Conversely, someone you think is way ahead of you is only a half-step in front.

The Inner Human Mechanism

We already have the equipment necessary to get us to where we want to go. The problem is, many of us don't believe it.

When expectations are set low, our determination diminishes.

Our internal computer is a superior machine. To operate at full capacity, it needs to be serviced properly. This requires a balance of a good diet, plenty of rest, and the right amount of stress to keep us aware and interested in everything going on in our lives. Maintaining a positive belief in yourself helps you to know you are loved and are worthy of anything you need and want.

The eternal battle within each of us, though, is our inner level of expectation. This level of expectation is guided by an internal steering mechanism which is developed throughout our lives by the opinions of others. Parents, teachers, friends, co-workers, siblings, and even strangers help establish our self-perception. It is based strictly on their opinions or perception of reality.

What really matters is our personal perception, not the perception of others. Their opinions often have nothing to do with us; they are drawn from their own life experiences and personal history. Oftentimes we will not even see the person again, but their negative review seeps deeply and we hold onto that opinion forever. It's important to understand that the person was merely speaking without consideration for our feelings or opinions. Despite knowing this, however, we may still be held back thinking we are unable to do any better, so why try? This is the problem, though. We tend to gravitate to our own internal level of expectation. When expectations are set low, our determination diminishes. We need to raise our level of expectation to reach for a higher goal.

This concept of positive self-image is rather new in the history of psychology. Surprisingly, it was an area of interest of a successful New York plastic surgeon. In the 1960s, Dr. Maxwell Maltz became fascinated by his patients' self-perception. This was a time when plastic surgery was usually reserved for reconstructive facial surgeries. Maltz noticed that although his work transformed people's physical appearances, some patients did not mentally respond to the work and continued to bemoan their self-image. Maltz studied these patients and authored the breakthrough book *Psycho-Cybernetics* based on his findings.

The word "cybernetic" comes from the Greek term "kybernetes," which means "steersman." Although it usually refers to how a computer or animal organizes itself to achieve a task, Maltz applied the science to humans to form "psycho-cybernetics." Maltz studied the concept that achievement was a matter of choice. More important to the dynamic of achieving is the "what" (the target), rather than the "how" (the path).

Each of us has this internal process, an inner steering mechanism. It is similar to a thermostat in a building. We set the thermostat to the desired temperature, and it signals the air-handling system (heating and cooling) to turn on as needed. Likewise, our level of expectation sets the "temperature" at which signals for action are triggered. As the conditions or situations and self-talk are monitored by our inner steering mechanism, we know when we are reaching the limit of what we can do or expect in our lives.

Maltz found that a minority of his patients didn't feel better about themselves after surgery. Though their outer appearance was repaired and reconstructed, inside their "deformity" continued to cause anguish. Without a change to this inner image, patients still felt themselves to be ugly, despite the excellence of the cosmetic work.

The interesting point about self-image is that it is valve neutral, meaning it doesn't care if it is empowering or destructive, but will simply form itself according to whatever psychological food it is fed. The beauty of self-image is that while it is the supreme factor in determining success or failure, it is also extremely malleable.

We need to consistently raise our level of expectation and work on maximizing strengths and minimizing weaknesses. One way to minimize our weaknesses is to change how we think about ourselves. Life doesn't just happen to us; we are participants. It's all about choices and how we respond, act, and react to every situation.

You are only as limited as your mind allows.

Our everyday choices determine whether we end up living a proactive or reactive life. Consistent choices form habits. Consciously consistent good choices form an extraordinary life. Conversely, consistently bad choices form bad habits. How we feel about ourselves and how we choose are connected. Even if we choose to do nothing, we have made a choice.

Napoleon Hill said it best in his classic book, Think and Grow Rich: "What the mind can conceive and believe it can achieve." You are only as limited as your mind allows. Everyone's dreams are achievable, but only if we are diligent enough to follow through with the desires of our heart. Successful people think of an idea and work toward implementing it. Success may require sacrifice and hard work, but by continually believing they can accomplish something, they will. Less successful people may have similar ideas, but they don't believe they are achievable. As a result of their thought process, the idea remains just that—an idea.

Your only limit is what you think you can achieve. You may have been told throughout your life that having dreams is a waste of time, to forget them and just focus on your job. Yet everything you encounter on a daily basis started as somebody's dream—staplers, remote controls, traffic lights, fast-food restaurants, mailing envelopes, toothpaste. The only difference is that those with the dream followed through until their idea was reality.

Imagination is key. The Greek definition of image is "to conceive." So when we imagine something, we are, in fact, conceiving an idea of what we want. Therefore, imaging an idea, or picture, in our mind is something we can work toward achieving. It is actually much deeper, though, because all we do is create. It is really about controlling what we create.

Every thought you have creates something. What needs to be controlled is whether the "creation" is positive or negative. You can think about your car. You may think it is great or awful. You may say, "I want a new car," but in your mind you may be saying, "I hate this old car and I want a new one." Your focus then is on your old car that you hate. You are in essence creating more of the old car that you hate rather than letting go of thoughts about your old car and creating the arrival of the new car you want.

When we want to create something new, we must take the picture of the car—or other thing desired—and add to it thoughts about *why* we want it. What benefits will we receive? With the example of the car, we may desire safe transportation. This action starts us on the road to achieving whatever it may be. Focusing on the picture of what we want and defining the thought process will propel us toward the goal. What we see is what we can get. The old Canon camera ads with Andre Agassi ring true: "Image is everything."

The lesson is that when used improperly, our thoughts limit us. Have you ever seen an exotic aquarium containing a shark? The shark is not a special breed but a typical shark that is limited in size because of its environment. As you know, sharks will grow in length to 6, 7, 8, 9 feet or longer in the ocean. But in an aquarium, they will only grow to a length suited to their surroundings. Many of us are limited by the small pool where we choose to swim. By expanding our desires, thoughts, and wishes—and then acting on them—we choose to swim in a larger pool and so we grow more.

Several life tenets have an effect on how we create our reality and live our lives. Making adjustments, many times in only a small way, produces tremendous results. Combine the process above with the tenets discussed below, and spiritual aspects discussed later, and you will be able to create an incredible life for yourself. These tenets are presented in no particular order. You might use all of them or merely a few. Simply consider implementing them in your life.

Potential

Think of potential as buried treasure hidden on the inside. We all have different and unique talents. Many of us have the ability to perform incredible feats with infinite potential. Though it may be good to have potential, it can also be detrimental. Potential becomes a dangerous concept when it keeps us stuck. Who has not thought at one time or another "One day I'm going to …" or "Once I get better at this, I will be able to …" or even "I just need a little more time to develop this." With thinking like that, we can never get to where we want to go. Ego often keeps us focused on the past or the future so we never realize how great life is *today*. Potential is for the present, not something to hold onto for the future.

For many years, I lived in the realm of potential. No achievement was ever good enough since I felt I had the potential to achieve so much more. I always believed it was in store at some future time, but that time never came. Once that building fell on me, I realized that I may not be around for that future success the ego dangled in front of me. You see, potential can sometimes be *Do not die with your dream still on the inside - allow yourself to be the shining star you know you are today.* nothing more than a cruel joke. Many of us are afraid today because we fear we are not living up to our potential. The funny thing is, there is no difference in potential if we allow life to happen today and truly enjoy it.

Do not die with your dream still on the inside. Rise up with confidence and boldness, and allow yourself to be the shining star you know you are today. Don't let the ego convince you that you aren't good enough right now. Take a step of faith and turn your potential into a desire. Many times, we are mired in the mud of an ill-conceived notion of who we really are. We choose to stay in the darkness because it represents the pain and limitation we already know. We are afraid to step out for fear of some new pain. Give yourself a break, and allow yourself to be who you are. This casts light on fear and pain to dissolve it. Give yourself permission to live up to or beyond your potential everyday. You'll be allowing yourself to blossom into an incredible human being.

Intention

The difference between success and failure is the power of intention. Desire means "to wish for; to crave." Intention, using a mathematical analogy, is desire to the 10th power. Intention is the spark within our soul that says, "I am going to do this. I am not going to stand for this anymore. I want this and I want it now!"

Desire leads to thoughts, which generate intention. The concept is drawn from quantum physics, which focuses on energy. Everything and every being is energy, vibrating at different levels. The level of vibrations we send out corresponds to the level of vibrations returning to us. A thought starts as energy, and the subconscious mind doesn't differentiate between our thoughts. Therefore, if we think negative thoughts and give them vibrations, they become our intentions.

You are a powerful, incredible, wonderful, and passionate human being. This is your true essence; yet many of us see ourselves as far less. Why do we spend our days focusing on what we cannot do, who we cannot be, the challenges we will not overcome, and the dreams we will not achieve? The answer lies in our intentions. Intention coupled with action has the ability to accomplish amazing results. Thoughts must be directed toward the result you truly want because you will get what you expect.

Use the power of intention to make positive changes in your life. It may not be as easy as it seems, but it's easier than you may think. No matter where you came from or what your current circumstances are, if you desire change badly enough and are willing to work hard enough, you will achieve your dreams through the power of intention.

The biggest problem we all face is answering the question, "What do I want?" What do we really want? The sad part is that most of us do not have a clue what our innermost desires are. We are too caught up in outside "noise" to keep our mind occupied, so we cannot figure out which way to go. We sit around waiting for divine inspiration. We hope that miraculously somehow, someway, this purpose will strike us like a bolt of lighting and we will become enlightened. Sadly, the result is putting off fully living your life while it slowly passes by. You will settle for less than you are capable of achieving, and the truly sad part is that you know this to be true. Tony Robbins, probably the most successful motivational speaker of his time, says, "It's the decisions and not your conditions that shape your destiny." It is your choice to be who you are and have what you have in your life.

Figure out your desire and develop a plan of intention. Without a plan, motivation may give you a warm and fuzzy feeling inside, but not much else. Too many people allow life to dictate their direction. They hesitate to make choices they know are in their best interest. They are just too afraid of the work necessary to achieve that change.

Some of us are so afraid of potential challenges that we miss the opportunity to grow. "Someday …" or "Well, maybe …" or "In a year or two …" just won't cut it. Challenges brought on by change await each of us. We will be shoved out of our comfort zones and forced to respond. We can respond positively or negatively, with hope and optimism or with resentment and negativism. Choose and hold a vision of what you want out of life and the Universe will help you make your vision a reality. Consciously make your choices and expect the Universe to help.

It is your choice to be who you are and have what you have in your life.

Developing a Plan

Once you have decided what it is you want, you need to plan how to achieve it. Did you know that most people spend more time planning a two-week vacation than they do planning how to achieve their goals? If you want to be as happy and content as you are for those two weeks skiing in the mountains or hanging out at the beach, you need to approach life just as thoroughly. Instead of stating, "I want to be fit, successful, or in love with a gorgeous mate," map out a route for reaching that goal. Even Columbus had a plan, as crazy as everyone else thought it was.

Let's say you want to lose 50 pounds in 12 months. While this is a healthy target, it's not specific enough to act upon. So break it down. Determine what it will take to achieve it. For example, to reach this goal, you'll have to cut 500 calories from your daily diet and start exercising. Suddenly, this insurmountable thing called "weight loss" becomes more viable. Thirty minutes of walking a day, fewer sodas ... you could do that.

Pick something bold and inspire yourself to reach for it. Break it down into detailed steps or sub-goals.

Use this same strategy for planning and reaching all your goals. Pick something bold and inspire yourself to reach for it. Break it down into detailed steps or sub-goals. To run a marathon, for instance, you will first train so you make it to the end of the street. Once this sub-goal is reached, you act on the next step toward a marathon.

This is the approach I used in regaining use of my legs. Once the doctors finally agreed to work at strengthening my leg muscles, I focused on sub-goals with walking being my ultimate goal. To begin building muscle, therapists placed dollies (small wooden squares with wheels attached) under my feet as I lay flat on my back. Moving the dollies and adding weight to them strengthened my leg muscles. Catching the beach ball targeted muscles needed for balance. This led to standing. Each sub-goal was a small target, but together they built on each other to allow me to achieve a larger goal.

Growth comes not only in learning how to develop a plan to ensure you'll reach goals, but for the transformation that takes place while achieving those goals. I was restless in the seemingly slow progress toward walking. But the energy and focus required did change me. I could never be the person I was before paralysis because that person could never have imagined living in a wheelchair or doing the work involved in leaving that wheelchair behind.

Setting goals provides purpose and direction. Goals allow you to make better decisions, and become more organized and effective, and they will give you greater confidence and self-worth. Setting goals is priceless; you only pay a price for not setting them. You can choose to get caught up in the everyday activity of life and let it lead you into a life without any real sense of purpose. Or you can choose to accomplish something meaningful with your life that gives you a sense of direction and purpose.

Did you know that only 3 percent of the US population sets goals, and less than half of those people write the goals down? *Become unique.* Define your purpose. The two major reasons people don't set goals for themselves are fear and the risk that the goal may not be attainable. Actually, setting goals and writing them down forces you to visualize your goals. Additionally, writing down goals creates a commitment.

There are many different levels of goals. Some are long-term or for achieving something big. Others are small, short-term, or stepping-stones toward a large-scale goal. Whatever the level, it's important to first decide what you want to do with your life and what large-scale goals you wish to achieve. From there, the goals are broken down into smaller and smaller targets. As you achieve each target, you'll ultimately achieve your life's dream.

Habits

First we create our habits, then they create us. Actually, that's good news because it means habits can be changed. Studies show that up to 90 percent of our normal behavior is based on the habits we develop. How difficult is it to create new habits? Research shows that habits can be reversed in as little as 21 days. When someone practices the same action each day for 21 consecutive days, a habit is formed. You can use this technique to form a habit or break unwanted and destructive patterns and replace them with a new habit or discipline.

We need to control the thoughts that occupy our mind. Emerson said, "We become what we think about all day long."

What prevents us from change? Since humans are born with only two fears—the fear of being dropped (or falling) and the fear of a loud noise—all other fears are learned. Family, friends, comfort, fear, and doubt all contribute to disrupting our attempts to change. Positive thoughts can counter these fears and obstacles.

A one-car garage can hold only one car. The same is true for thoughts. The mind can only hold one thought at a time. If we tune into what we are thinking, we can discipline our thoughts. This aids us in reversing bad and unwanted habits and creating new ones. The mind becomes a battlefield for change. Humans have 50,000 thoughts each day. If we're not aware of our thoughts, we can get sucked into someone else's thought process. For example, advertising and television influence our thoughts. Watching the news, with all its horrific stories, causes stress. But then the commercial features a pill that will calm you down. Late-night ads for breakfast food make you hungry and entice you to overeat. Subliminal advertising works because its messages bypass our conscious mind and go directly to our subconscious. Our conscious mind often wanders, allowing subconscious thoughts to enter unnoticed.

We need to control the thoughts that occupy our mind. Emerson said, "We become what we think about all day long." Our thought life is responsible for our circumstances, but we choose which thoughts we entertain. Take advantage of this method for your own good by sowing good thought seeds and reaping the physical manifestation. Continue to think in positive ways and outline or establish what you want out of life. By continually doing that, the subconscious mind will begin to bring people and events into your life to make it happen. It works for me. It worked in recovering from my accident and in producing this book. I know it can work for you. Our thoughts create our habits, and habits ultimately create our reality.

Perseverance & Hard Work

Once you make a decision to do something, you must commit to do whatever is necessary to achieve the result. Establish in your mind that you have no other option. This is perseverance; it allows you to see things through.

We often decide we would like to do something but give up once we encounter the first obstacle. We may set out with good intentions, but inevitably outside distractions creep in and we drift from our goal. If we remain focused on our goal and persevere through any difficulties, we will achieve success.

I get distracted, too, but I continually reevaluate my goals. This allows me to step back, refocus, and correct my course. Goals can change, and so can the paths or directions we take to reach them. Constant attention, the ability to make adjustments, and opening to inner growth will all help you succeed beyond your expectations.

In addition to setting and focusing your goal, you need to believe you can accomplish it. This is what I faced while working with Sonia to strengthen my legs. But establishing a desire and creating a plan to achieve it is actually the easy part. You must now make the journey. And perseverance will carry you through to the end.

There were many periods of monotony in doing the exercises to rebuild my leg and abdominal muscles so I would be physically ready to stand—and finally to walk. Without perseverance, I would not have succeeded. Sonia and everyone else who helped me reach my goal could not take action or follow through for me. That was up to me and me alone. Perseverance is what separates successful people from everyone else. You need to remain consistent and resolved to succeed, even if others are telling you that you cannot do it, that you will fail.

I have spent a great deal of my life doing things because others said I could not. If I listened to all the medical people after my accident, I'd probably still be sitting in a wheelchair. No matter what obstacle or naysayer you encounter, persevere as if there is no other alternative. Keep working toward your goal, your purpose, and you will succeed. Do not let the fear of failure kill your passion and your dreams.

Hard work ensures reaching your goals. I am all for working smarter, but I do not know anyone who has become a success without having to work for it. The employee who goes the extra mile is typically the first to get a raise and is the last to be out of a job. This principle is true no matter what your goal is because the energy you put forth is bound to come back. It's not always the best-looking person who finds a great relationship, nor the person with the seemingly greatest advantages who ultimately succeeds. It's the person with a passion and a desire for the day-to-day accomplishments—who holds as high a value for the journey as for the results—who exceeds his goal.

The adage is true; you do reap what you sow. But make sure the right seed is planted in good soil.

The adage is true; you do reap what you sow. But make sure the right seed is planted in good soil. Be a giver, not a getter. Give all that you have for your vision. The getters of the world appear to win for a short time but ultimately lose. The givers win long before any prize is evident to others.

I admit that I am human and sometimes struggle to get what I want. Life doesn't put everything we want on a silver platter. God will work with us to get the silver platter, but it is a co-creative effort. Whatever you choose to do with your life, do it with all your might. Work hard and success will follow.

People have often wondered how I get results in life, how I am able to handle things. While there may be a number of contributing factors, the real reason is that I never, ever give up. This is one of my deep beliefs and convictions. It's how I recovered from paralysis. At times, it required a tenacious faith within to hold on—no matter what.

Succeeding in that goal deepened my perseverance for the next. I remain focused on what my end desire is, and I believe there is always a way.

Many times those around me have doubted my ideas, but more often than not, what seemed irrational and impossible was doable. You've heard the old saying, "Where there is a will, there is a way." If it's in your heart to do something, you can do it. When you truly believe you can do something, the Universe (God) is delighted to guide you in getting it done. That doesn't mean it will be easy. It means you can accomplish it as long as you are committed to completing your goal.

Attitude

You are what you think. If you think you will, you will. If you think you won't, you won't. It's as simple as that. Throughout history, famous people have been quoted about attitude and the thought processes. Jesus tells us, "As you think, so shall you be." Abraham Lincoln said, "People are about as happy as they make up their mind to be." Henry David Thoreau wrote, "If one advances confidently in the direction of his dreams, and endeavors to live the life which he has imagined, he will meet with a success unexpected in common hours." It's attitude that determines your perception of reality.

I'm not saying this is a sugar-coated gumdrop world where thinking positively ensures everything will be okay. Nor am I looking at this from an overly simplistic point of view. What I am saying is that you need to train your mind to respond in a positive manner. A defeatist attitude arises out of questions such as "Why me? Why does this always happen to me?" Thoughts can linger on blaming others and insisting you could have had a different life if only these bad things didn't happen all the time. However, when your questions force you to consider action, your thoughts shift toward the positive. "What can I do about this?" or "How can I make this work to my advantage?" are questions that provide the power to change your circumstances.

I've had some bad moments, but never a bad day.

I can honestly say that no matter what happens to me in life, I don't ask, "Why me?" I still may be hurt, or upset, or stunned by current circumstances, but my immediate mental response is always "What can I do about this?" Whenever somebody asks me how I am doing, 99 percent of the time I inevitably answer, "Never had a bad day." I cannot quote some of the responses I get back, but I always follow up with "I've had some bad moments, but never a bad day."

Practice responding to negative thoughts by turning them into positive responses. It eventually becomes an effortless habit. In spite of my upbringing, I was able from an early age to always look at the positive side of things. Today, no matter what happens, I always look at the positive and what I can accomplish from any given circumstance.

Is change hard? You bet it is. If it were easy, everybody would be doing it! Most people give in to short-term pleasures rather than holding off for long-term progress. They don't stop to think that they pay a higher price for giving in to short-term gratification. Stay the course and hold out for the long-term possibilities. Don't let today's frustrations eliminate tomorrow's opportunities.

Assertiveness

This was a hard trait for me to master. During my childhood, I was terribly shy and afraid to ask for anything. As I grew older, I saw that if I didn't ask for what was mine, I would rarely get it. Still, it was difficult to be assertive. Handled properly, assertiveness provides benefits for everyone. Assertiveness is asking for what you want. The Bible instructs, "Ask and you shall receive, seek and you shall find, knock and it shall be opened unto you."

So what stops us from asking for what we want? Typically, it's one of three things:

1. Our belief system says it's not right to ask.
2. We lack confidence.
3. We fear rejection.

However, at some point, we need to take a leap of faith—and that means releasing old beliefs, feeling good about ourselves, and understanding that even though the world is perfect in how things work, it is not Utopia.

Assertiveness is asking for what we want without bullying others to get it. Otherwise, how we act with others can be a considerable source of stress in our lives. Becoming assertive can actually reduce stress since we stand up for our legitimate rights without pushing others around or allowing them to abuse us. It's important to understand that there's enough of everything for everyone. We don't need to take anything away from anyone else to get what we want. *There is plenty.* By asking and receiving, we allow the Universe (God) to bring what we want to us. It was always ours and was never intended to belong anywhere else.

A person is considered assertive when they stand up for their rights in such a way that the rights of others are not violated.

Assertiveness was initially identified as a personality trait by Andrew Salter in 1949. The premise at the time was that some people had it while others did not, just like extroversion or stinginess. By the late 1950s and into the 1960s, assertiveness was redefined as one's ability to express personal rights and feelings. Psychologists found that people could be assertive in some situations yet totally ineffectual in others.

A person is considered assertive when they stand up for their rights in such a way that the rights of others are not violated. It has nothing to do with demanding our rights. Assertive people can express their personal likes and interests spontaneously, they can talk about themselves without being self-conscious, they can disagree with the opinions of others, and they are able to say "No." In short, when we are assertive, we are more relaxed in interpersonal situations because our words and actions are not an attack on others. Assertive people don't insist on changing the perceptions of others or impinge on the rights of the people around them.

Studies done in the 1970s found that some unassertive people felt that they didn't have the right to be assertive. Additionally, some said that they didn't think all people were equal, and they rejected the idea that all should be treated equally. In most instances, this type of trait developed in childhood. In my childhood situation, I had a skewed thought process and didn't think I deserved things. I certainly paid a price for that. I, and many others like me, grew up doubting ourselves and looking to others for validation and guidance.

While you didn't have much of a choice about what you were taught as a child, you do have the option of deciding whether to continue behaving according to poor assumptions (if that is what you were taught). If this was your experience, continuing to cling to those assumptions will keep you from being an assertive adult. You are the best judge of your thoughts, feelings, wants, needs, and behavior. Nobody is better informed than you are as to how and why you got where you are today. As a result, you're the best person for expressing your position on many important issues. Because we are all unique individuals, there are times when we differ significantly with others in our lives. Rather than overpower the meek or give in to the aggressive, you have the right to express your position and try to negotiate your differences. As you become more assertive, you begin to lay claim to your right to relax and are able to take time for yourself.

How assertive we are relates to our interpersonal style—how we interact with others. Three basic interpersonal styles are outlined below. Which represents your current style? If needed, consider what you can do to become a more well-rounded human being.

The first type is the *aggressive style*. This person tends to fight, accuse, threaten, and generally step on other people without regard for their feelings. The advantage to this type of behavior is that these people usually don't get pushed around. The disadvantage is that people usually don't want to be around them.

The extreme opposite of the aggressive personality is the *passive style*. This person doesn't stand up for himself and allows others to push to him around. They do what they are told, regardless of how it feels. The advantage to this style of interaction is that they rarely experience direct rejection because they buckle to the demands of others. The disadvantage is that they're taken advantage of and also build up tremendous amounts of resentment and anger.

The final style, falling between these other two extremes, is the *assertive personality*. A person with this style doesn't allow others to push them around. At the same time, they consider the feelings of others. The advantage of this style is that they usually get what they want without making others mad. By being assertive, we can act in our own best interests and not feel guilty about it.

You'll know that you're behaving assertively when you are standing up for yourself and expressing your true feelings. When you master this type of behavior, you need not worry about being withdrawn. You don't need to lash out and attack others, and there's no need for blame. The easiest way to strike a balance in this style is to admit that aggressive or passive styles will fail to get you what you want. There is no disadvantage in using this style.

Balance

Is your life in balance? I know this may sound like a simple question, but many of us burn the candle too much in one area of our lives while ignoring other equally important aspects. Then, when something blows up in a place we're neglecting, we wonder how it could have possibly happened. Is your career going strong, your income soaring, yet you don't have time to enjoy it? If this is the case, you're probably out of balance.

If your hobbies and activities are taking time away from your family and friends, you're out of balance. If you're so busy with other things that you are ignoring your health, you need a balance adjustment. If you have the house on the beach, the luxury car, and the boat, yet no one to enjoy them with, you're definitely out of balance.

Sigmund Freud said, "Being entirely honest with one's self is a good idea." Well, if you're truly honest with yourself about this, you'll see where you may be out of balance. You can then take the steps necessary to correct it. In *The 7 Habits of Highly Effective People,* Stephen Covey talks about sharpening the sword to strike a balance in your life. He discusses the balance among the physical, mental, social/emotional, and spiritual areas of your life. When you spend too much time in one given sector (say your career), it impacts other areas of your life, such as family or your physical condition. Humans are in an optimal state when all parts of their life are in balance. Do you currently have a balanced life, or is it concentrated in one particular arena?

From a personal perspective, I swore at an early age that I was going to be a success no matter the cost. As a young adult, I saw a bumper sticker on a car that read, "He who dies with the most toys wins." It became my motto. I focused entirely on my career, forsaking everything else. When I found myself in a difficult work situation, it would consume me because I had nothing else to balance it out. I often left that position to find something I felt was a better fit. When this behavior became a pattern, I decided to start my own business so I could control my situation even more. My entire life was wrapped up in the business 24/7. *And I mean 24/7.* I spent any free time I had alone because I didn't develop outside interests.

I believe this is why, aside from the physical injuries, the accident was so devastating. It forced me to look at myself and my current life situation. How could I be on this earth merely to run a business? There had to be more to life. From the ashes of the aftermath of the accident arose a different me—one seeking my true purpose in life. As I've mentioned, the change didn't occur overnight; it took many years of subtle nudges to get me in the direction I'm headed today. Yes, I do currently own a business, but my life is so much richer—not necessarily in terms of financial riches, but in a balance I've never experienced before. I still have to force myself to make adjustments from time to time; I didn't say I was perfect.

Perhaps intuitively, successful individuals throughout time have known the importance of having balance in their lives.

Have you ever felt your life was out of control? If you have, you probably have a problem in balancing life's priorities. Balance is the type of thing that sounds good in theory but is hard to apply in real life. With the constant demands from our work and families, it may be difficult to imagine a life that allows for all the things you would like to do. Many people make the mistake of putting other people's needs ahead of their own. This, however, may be a costly mistake in the long run. Burnout, depression, and loss of health are often the price we pay for not making balance a priority in our lives.

Perhaps intuitively, successful individuals throughout time have known the importance of having balance in their lives. Instead of living to work, they worked to live. In the process, they became more well-rounded and balanced individuals. These are all characteristics that certainly correlate to success. The easiest way I have found to check whether I'm in balance is to occasionally step back and feel what's happening inside of me. Am I stressed? Anxious? Fearful? It's times like these when we need to take stock of our current situation. Is every sector of our lives in balance or are we consumed by one particular area? Chances are, if we feel happy inside, the parts of our life are in sync. Learn to listen to how you're feeling. It's how we know what's going on and what's missing. Your inner knowing is trying to tell you something.

Procrastination

This has been an Achilles' heel for me. If I don't feel like doing something, or if it doesn't get my juices flowing, I will procrastinate getting it done. Yet procrastination can make the difference between success and failure. Success develops out of the details, so it's important to give them the necessary time and attention.

Procrastination is a habit, nothing more. It certainly is not a fatal flaw. It takes persistence to change, but it can be done.

In my work, I always carry a tablet with lists of things re-

Two Steps for Ending Procrastination

Do you want to change, quit procrastinating, and get moving? Here's how. First, think about your goals. It may help to write them out. Then post them all around so you are continually reminded of what you really want to do. When developing your goals, make sure you know that they're something you should do and that they're very important to you. If your actions don't align with your intentions, you'll have a recipe for disaster instead of a plan for success.

Second, learn to manage your time more effectively. If you don't know how, learn how. Seek out someone who you admire for their success. Ask them how they do it and mimic their actions and attitudes. One way to manage your time more efficiently is to break goals into smaller, more attainable tasks. Make a list of everything you must do to accomplish a goal.

quired for each project. It helps define what's necessary to make each project successful. After each task is completed, I strike it off the list. What an empowering feeling that can be! Conversely, things constantly arise that must be added to the list. It is an ebb and flow. I have found such a list to be a specific way to get things done, stop procrastination, and become successful. It's similar to grocery shopping. If you take a list, you purchase what you need. If you don't, you'll wander around the store gathering items but then return home only to realize all the things you forgot. Lists keep you on target.

It also helps to become better organized. A disorganized lifestyle doesn't allow for much success. Organize your environment with everything you'll need so it will be easier to get things accomplished. If you're a major procrastinator, you will not eliminate this habit overnight. It takes practice, persistence, and dedication, but you can do it! Start out small and build gradually. How does a mouse eat an elephant? One bite at a time. If your procrastination has become an elephant, then get yourself moving today—one small piece at a time.

For some, it helps to have an attitude change. Don't allow a self-defeating attitude to stop you from creating the life you want. Replace self-defeating thoughts with self-enhancing thoughts. Don't think of everything as "all or nothing." Instead, remember the idea of breaking each situation into small pieces of a greater plan. Many times, when we procrastinate, we end up blaming ourselves for not being able to move forward. This blocks us further from getting things done. Instead, we need to remind ourselves of the consequences if we procrastinate, as well what will happen if we begin to move forward.

Try this if you tend to procrastinate. Close your eyes for a moment and visualize yourself as a non-procrastinating person. Imagine how much you will accomplish. Imagine the stress melting away because you no longer have to worry about not doing something. Remember how good it feels to take action. Now start to behave in this new way, even if only for a few moments at a time. Also, learn from your mistakes and don't judge them. Judging them leads to the propensity to beat yourself up and ultimately makes you a bigger procrastinator than you may already be.

For some, it helps to engage a friend or family member. We all benefit at times from an outside opinion or another way to look at a situation. Find someone who has your best interests at heart. You'll then know that they will listen to you and share in the successes, as well as the setbacks. Don't share with everyone. Some people in your life actually prefer that you fail and will only advise you to give up. Let supportive people help you get your thoughts in order and aid you in moving in a positive direction. In those times when you are moving forward, use impulsiveness to your advantage—act when ideas pop into your head.

Learn to become successful on the inside first. When you do that, it will show itself to the world.

We are all unique, incredible individuals. Yet we each also have our faults or, more specifically, what we consider to be our weaknesses. This is what being human is all about. Procrastination may be a euphemism for whatever we may perceive our shortcomings to be. But we need to learn to accept ourselves for who we are. We must understand that sometimes things do not work out as quickly as we had hoped. We need to learn to give ourselves credit for anything we do. We need to learn to forgive ourselves—and forgive ourselves a lot. Remember that being a success has nothing to do with what you do; rather, it is about who you are. Learn to become successful on the inside first. When you do that, it will show itself to the world.

Patience

People who know me tell me I have the patience of Job. At times, I cringe when I hear that because I know I don't. Other times, I cringe because I know I don't want to be so patient. I want the same instant results and gratification that our society has come to expect. I also realize that my patience has served me well as it has become more refined over the years. Our experience is all about the choices we make. When you can step outside of your experience for a moment and watch it unfold, you have the ability to make the choices best suited for you. This requires patience, since too often we want instant responses to our requests. *I know I do.* But it's the ability to allow things to happen that places us in synchronicity and flow.

We develop patience by having to wait or agonize over the outcome of a situation that we have no control over. It's in these moments when we refine the ability to be patient. As we do, we learn not to worry or be anxious. Patience allows Universal Intelligence to provide us with the answers we need when we are ready to listen.

The first step in acquiring patience is to look within. What do you truly want out of life? We could all know the answer if we searched our heart, but many of us never take the time. Navigating in a way that's authentic for us aligns our inner-self with the Universe and what the Universe has destined for us to accomplish. In the long run, it allows us to find our truth. We respond to every present moment and discover how it affects our desires. Focusing on the present, and staying there, allows us fulfillment in each moment along the way. We need not focus on some future moment that may or may not arrive.

When we focus on the future, it's easy to get frustrated. We can feel such a huge sense of separation between where we want to be versus where we are now. This may make us give up on the journey. I was so focused in my business, thinking someday I would be able to sit back and enjoy the fruits of my labor, that the fear of the present moment became a great divide. I forced myself to work harder in the present for fear I would never reach my future—the place I wanted to be. It was a vicious cycle. I was like a hamster on a wheel. No matter how fast I ran, I remained at the same spot on the wheel.

Good things can come out of a building falling on you. Once you get over the initial shock, you are forced to reevaluate your perceptions and perspectives. Now, even though there may be times when I'm anxious, I live to the best of my ability moment to moment knowing the Universe (God) has my best interests at heart.

Focus on your dreams and desires. Focus on listening to the inner voice we all have. Stop trying to drown it out with all the noise of life. That will only lead you astray. Learn to listen to that voice; it will guide you to be in the right place at the right time. As this guidance develops, you learn awareness and understand that patience is at work to bring you to your higher good. You'll be amazed at the synchronicity that will become commonplace in your life. Get quiet, be still, listen carefully, and be ready for your success to happen.

Fear

Spirituality believes that we are all connected as one through a Universal Intelligence of source energy. This connection is pure love (God). Fear is the separation from love. *A Course in Miracles* states:

Nothing real can be threatened.
Nothing unreal exists.
Herein lies the peace of God.

It is further noted in the book, *"The opposite of love is fear, but what is all-encompassing can have no opposite."*

From a secular position, we might say that fear is being in the unknown. The ego needs to be in control, and it cannot control the unknown. The result is fear, which may manifest itself as anger, resistance, or putting life on hold. Yet some of the greatest triumphs in our lives happen when we step out into the unknown and find growth.

When we are not in a place where we feel or recognize love, we experience fear. It can show up in many forms—lack, pain, anger, or violence—but they all represent fear. We also have a choice. We can choose to experience the fear or see the truth in any given situation. Many times, when we see the truth, we find that we had nothing to fear to begin with. Transform fear into faith: faith within yourself, faith that your situation will work out fine, faith that you are protected, and faith that you are loved.

Transform fear into faith: faith within yourself, faith that your situation will work out fine, faith that you are protected, and faith that you are loved.

Use inner growth as a guidepost to alleviate fear. Think back to a time when you experienced tremendous fear. Something positive had to come out of that situation. So consider how it turned out. What was positive about it? You obviously did not die. What strength do you now know that you acquired from that situation? Look for a lesson you may have learned through that experience.

Our fear often comes from a childhood experience. I know my mother lived her entire life in fear, and as a child, I became neurotic from feeding off that negative fearful energy. There were many times my mother was so afraid to go somewhere that she would begin to exhibit symptoms of physical illness. I learned to experience the same thing. Perhaps some of your fears are due to a similar experience. If so, it's time for you to live your life *for you*—not for anybody else.

Were you blamed when you made a mistake or made to feel guilty? Simply let go of that pain and fear. Make a choice to stop playing the blame game. It's time to move on. Once you realize who you truly are and accept total responsibility for where you are right now in your life, you will be overcome by an incredible feeling of empowerment. Remember, *you are in charge* of you and your experience to date. Letting go is part of the extraordinary cleansing experience.

Allow yourself to be who you truly are. There's no need to hide from others, fearful of what they may think. None of us is perfect. This is why they put erasers on pencils. Besides, you'll be amazed at where you can go once you let go of the old ways of thinking about yourself.

Forgiveness & Gratitude

Too often we hold onto our hurts. For instance, sometimes we think we are within our rights to hold onto a grudge and be miserable. We deny ourselves the opportunity to experience love within ourselves when we do this. The only person we need to forgive is ourselves. When we cannot forgive someone for what we perceive to be a transgression, we only hurt ourselves. Forgiving doesn't mean accepting what has happened to us. It doesn't mean accepting unacceptable behavior either. It doesn't mean we have to become friends with someone who has hurt us. Instead, forgiving is part of the process of letting go. The longer we hold resentment toward another, the longer we are bound to them. By forgiving, we learn that we are able to move on with our lives. The funny part is that in many situations, the person we are upset with doesn't even know they are the object of our scorn. Sometimes our grudges are even against people who are dead. Who benefits from that?

Quit holding onto the pain. I lived for many years with a rather extensive list of people who I felt had hurt me. I held

The longer we hold resentment toward another, the longer we are bound to them.

onto the pain, anger, and resentment for too many years. Once I decided to release the pain, the resentment began melting away. I saw unlimited potential as to what I could accomplish and who I could become.

Use empathy to aid in forgiving. When I was leaving the Magee Center, I felt both excited and apprehensive. I also experienced some guilt. Though I'd worked hard and come so far, I also wondered why I was able to walk out and the friends I'd made there would likely remain in wheelchairs. Until I accepted my situation and released my anxieties, I struggled in finding the blessings in the situation. When I considered the feelings of my friends from Magee, I felt conviction that miracles were available to others as well as me. What I mean by that is that I was no one special. There are opportunities for everyone, and I didn't get any special treatment from life for the ability to walk out of the hospital.

When we feel someone is hurting us, it benefits us to stop and think about how hurt this individual must feel. Usually, it's not even about us; it is about them and the pain they are experiencing in their own life. It may not even be intentional. You may perceive the situation in a tone reflecting your own mood at the time. When you see things in this light, it becomes easier to forgive. Forgiveness is an act of the heart. Just as the hurt you feel was never about you, the forgiveness you experience is never about them.

Having an attitude of gratitude clears the way for more good to come into our lives. No matter what trials and tribulations you're experiencing, you have many things to be grateful for. Show gratitude for even the smallest details. I promise you it will assist you in getting out of your suffering. Every morning when I wake up, I am immediately grateful for two things. First, I am grateful that I woke up. Second, I am grateful that once my feet touch the floor, I have the ability to walk. Some mornings, the pain from an occasional arthritis flare-up can be quite uncomfortable. However, because I am grateful for the ability to walk, it helps to offset the pain in some small way. With these two things to be grateful for, anything else that happens during the day is an added bonus. Finally, when I lay my head on the pillow at night, at a minimum I'm grateful for the opportunity to think of all the great things I experienced that day.

If you tend to look at the negative side of life, why not try it my way for a change? Other than your negativity, what have you got to lose?

Chapter 6

The Three Levels of Mind

WE ALL HAVE WHAT ARE KNOWN AS THREE levels of mind: *conscious*, *subconscious*, and *super conscious*. I've discussed them briefly as they relate to the basic life tenets. However, it's important to have a deeper understanding. Knowing how the mind works, especially how the three levels of mind operate both independently and with each other, allows us to focus more on what we wish to be our reality. First, we'll discuss the conscious and the subconscious mind and how they interrelate, then we'll discuss the super conscious mind.

Conscious Mind

The *conscious mind* is our analytical or thinking mind. It is the level we use while awake. It analyzes data, in conjunction with our five senses, and develops a theory and makes a judgment about an issue or situation. It then takes this information and stores it in the subconscious mind. The conscious mind will draw it out later when a situation of a similar nature arises in the future. It has to contend with previously stored information relating to whatever topic we are contemplating at any given time, almost like a computer.

For example, suppose you have an irrational prejudice toward someone, *anyone*. Let me give you a childhood example that affected me well into my adulthood. I am not proud of this example. My family moved to a new town when I was in the middle of the fourth grade. Since I was an extremely shy child, starting a new school in the middle of the year was quite scary. For whatever reason, I acclimated reasonably well and got along with the other kids quickly. There was a girl in the class who had bright red hair and so many freckles that it appeared she had freckles on top of freckles. She was teased by her classmates for this. She took a liking to me and would tell everybody in the class that she was going to marry me when we grew up. I received my share of teasing for being her "boyfriend." I was mortified. Because of this episode, I stayed away from redheaded girls through college and afterward. I passed up opportunities to date redheaded women that could have been wonderful experiences. Because of what happened back in fourth grade, I developed a prejudice completely blown out of proportion.

The sad part is that through prejudices (which many of us experience about one type of person or another), we miss out on some of the best relationships we could ever hope to have. I'm not talking only about intimate relationships, but friends, mentors, or the messengers the Universe (God) has sent to you with a solution to your problem.

The interesting, yet terribly sad thing about the above scenario is that if the same woman dyed her hair and then approached me, I would have reacted completely differently, though nothing changed but her hair color. Not every prejudice is that easy to resolve, but they are all just as superficial. Many are merely someone else's prejudice adopted as our own because we want to be accepted by our peers. The worst case is when we continue to hold onto those prejudices long after those friends are gone from our lives simply because they have become a habit.

The conscious mind exists in the present and nowhere else. It is affected strongly by the opinions of others and can quite easily have an effect on what is the best course for us. It separates everything into black/white, either/or categories. Because the conscious mind is analytical, it can see many possible solutions to any given situation. Ultimately, it doesn't have the ability to decide which course of action is best on its own and always checks with the subconscious mind before any decision is made. As a result, the conscious mind is often the source of indecision and can generate irrational thoughts. It's important to learn how to let go of these thoughts. Above is one example of how you can do this.

Clearing Out Irrational Thoughts

The next time you have an irrational thought about someone you don't even know, stop and ask yourself why. Listen to your answer, understand why the thought is irrational, and decide not to feel that way anymore. Each time you recognize that same feeling, make a conscious effort to think good thoughts about that type of person until a positive reaction becomes automatic. This process can also be used for other types of irrational thinking.

Subconscious Mind

The subconscious mind is like a giant file cabinet in our heads. Every experience we've ever had can be found in the subconscious mind. This level of mind actually helps determine our response or behavior in any given situation. It constantly stores information from our experiences and continues to provide the same "answers" until it has been re-programmed. No areas of gray exist in the subconscious mind. Everything is either black or white in order to provide a picture of reality based on what has been programmed into the subconscious. In other words, it functions based on our prior life experiences. Typically, when we dream at night, we are operating on the subconscious level. This area of the mind is much like a filter between the conscious mind and the super conscious (spiritual) mind. Whereas the conscious mind tends to act in an analytical manner, the subconscious mind operates from an emotional perspective.

Have you ever pushed somebody's buttons and gotten an explosive emotional response? Who has not done that before? The emotional reaction you receive is the irrational behavior that is linked to the person's subconscious response to that type of situation. They draw on prior experience pulled from the subconscious, whether it is their perspective on religion, politics, or the "history" of a given situation.

Research provides another interesting fact about the subconscious mind. Unlike the conscious mind, which works in linear time, for the subconscious mind *time doesn't really matter*. In fact, time seems to be irrelevant and will expand or shrink according to its needs.

The subconscious mind continuously receives a variety of information to sort out in order to respond to any situation. It gets advice from the super conscious mind on one side (spiritual) and draws judgments and analytical analysis from the conscious mind on the other side. In another sense, this level of mind is the battle between one's true self and the ego to gain control or at least influence our decisions. When the internal input doesn't agree, the battle to reconcile between the two begins. We can actually be fooled by the subconscious mind, thinking we are getting intuitive assistance when we may merely be receiving past experiences and our impressions of them.

Connecting the Conscious & the Subconscious

Every human being has the cognitive power of self-consciousness. We all have a sense of being aware of our experiences, as well as recognizing that we are conscious beings. With an awareness of our own conscious process, we are given the freedom and ability to make choices. The choices we make ultimately determine our perception of events or reality. What we believe about life mirrors back to us as our experiences.

In the brain stem, we find a bundle of nerves that is called the *Reticular Activating System (RAS)*. The RAS controls our awareness and arousal. Our ability to perceive, to think, and to respond to outside stimuli depends upon the RAS to correspond with the cortex of the brain. The cortex cannot wake itself up unless the RAS is in an aroused state. The RAS also controls our perception of outside things in relation to those within our inner world. In other words, the RAS acts as a middleman between the conscious mind and the subconscious mind. It takes direction from the conscious mind and passes this information on to the subconscious mind.

You have the ability to decide what is filtered between the conscious and subconscious mind by using your thoughts.

From a psychological perspective, the RAS corresponds to the ego. As infants, we are taught by our parents and then by teachers, siblings, and peers belief patterns that may not actually be true. The RAS responds to what we have been taught to believe as the truth, regardless of whether it is.

You have the ability to decide what is filtered between the conscious and subconscious mind by using your thoughts. If you don't like the results you have been receiving, you have the amazing ability to change your thought process and therefore your results. Pruning away negative thought patterns will reprogram the RAS to respond to outside stimuli with positive results. You choose the message from your conscious mind. The subconscious mind is merely a file cabinet of every experience you've ever had. Align it with what you want, not what others have taught you to want. You and you alone are in charge of your life.

Super Conscious Mind

Some call this *Unconscious Mind, Personal Spirit,* or *Universal Intelligence.* Whatever you choose to call this, it exists. Intuition and the ability to receive clarity exist within the super conscious mind. Whereas the conscious mind is limited by its analytical nature, the super conscious mind sees everything as part of the whole. It can, therefore, clearly see solutions where none may have existed before. The super conscious mind doesn't seem to exert any power over the conscious or subconscious mind. Rather, it appears to be an inner light often showing up in our subconscious mind during dreams as solutions or symbols to answer inner questions we are pondering. The super conscious mind has the ability to access every bit of information between our conscious mind and our subconscious mind. It can also pull in information from outside the human mind. This is why some refer to it as Universal Intelligence.

So how do we tap into this source contained within the super conscious mind? The easy answer is to never lie to yourself and to be true to your inner being. Have you ever thought about calling someone, perhaps a spouse or close friend, and because you are so well attuned, your phone rings and it's the person you were thinking of on the other end? Or if your phone didn't ring, you would call them and their response would be, "I was thinking of calling you." It happens to me regularly. When it first started happening, it would freak me out. Now, at times, when I want to speak with someone, I will focus that thought in my super conscious mind and wait for my phone to ring. It works!

At times, when you're with other like-minded people vibrating at a high frequency level, the combined super conscious minds will form into an even higher level of mind that all may access. This can allow for the creation of some incredible ideas. I know from a personal level, when I am focused on a goal, answers to problems and ideas I normally never thought of will pop into my mind at just the right time to assist me along the way. The super conscious mind will continually, without fail, solve every problem we encounter. The critical point to remember here is that the goal must be clear.

Also keep in mind that the answers provided may come in the form of problems to overcome, setbacks, or even temporary failure. In every problem, setback, or failure are valuable lessons to uncover. Another important aspect to remember is to remain calm and have an attitude of faith or belief. When you remain centered, the super conscious mind kicks in and will lead the way. I cannot tell you how many times, in the face of adversity and despair, I have believed and maintained my faith and then experienced answers appearing to resolve the problem with the best possible solution.

I cannot tell you how many times, in the face of adversity and despair, I have believed and maintained my faith and then experienced answers.

This happened many times before I even studied and believed in spiritual matters. Now that I have learned to open up to my super conscious mind, it happens even faster. This is because I now know that I have to listen and look for it to happen, and then be willing to accept it. It can happen for everyone, every time.

I'll share a personal example of how this works—and the example I am about to give you occurred before I even knew it worked. In the 1990s, two business partners and I were building homes in New Jersey. In 1995, we got involved in a land deal that was the biggest we had ever undertaken. We also had a land partner who was not the most honorable of people. In any event, by the summer of 1996, we began having cash-flow problems. The real problem was that we didn't know how deeply it extended. By the fall of that year, we realized that we were almost a million dollars in debt. Granted, the money was in the ground, but the market was slow, and if we didn't generate sales, we were going to generate ourselves into bankruptcy.

This was also the same time when I was evolving in my inner growth. One of my partners and I prayed over our despondency to perhaps find a way out of the wilderness. Our options consisted of selling off the ground and hopefully walking away broke (but even), or to convince everyone, including ourselves, to work through it and come out the other side. We really had no choice. I didn't want to give up and go work for someone else. Besides, the housing market was slow and no one was hiring. With no money in the bank, and receivables already extended out to as much as 120 days, this crazy idea came over us to work through it. Industry standards in our part of the country at the time were typically payment with 30 days.

What did "working through it" entail? It meant bringing in every tradesperson, sitting them down, explaining face-to-face the dire situation, and then asking them to continue to work with us. We needed to keep building but also needed to generate sales to get money to pay them. They had the option to quit. We promised them that if they did quit, they would still be paid for existing work, and no slower than if they stayed working with us. It also meant sitting down with our biggest supplier to ask for help. When we defined and focused on our goal, the Universe (God) took over. Our major supplier not only continued working with us, but loaned us an additional $100,000 to cover other expenses so we could keep going. I think only one, maybe two subcontractors stopped working for us. They were still paid off as we went along.

Additionally, our market began to pick up, which meant more sales. Of course, we experienced setbacks along the way. However, our belief in our plan and, more importantly, belief in ourselves kept us moving forward. Every step along the way, an answer appeared out of nowhere at just the right time. Within one year—a mighty hard year, I might add—we had paid off all our back debts and were $250,000 in the black!

Tapping the Super Conscious

The super conscious mind is quietly very powerful. The following steps will help you connect with a super-conscious mind response:

1. Sit down and get quiet.
2. Wait for a response that comes from your heart.
3. Be certain what you're asking for is clear.
4. If no answer comes immediately, be patient—it will appear.
5. Remain calm.
6. Once you receive intuitive intelligence—act upon it immediately.

Chapter 7

Reinforced Understanding

I AM AN EXTREMELY LEFT-BRAINED INDIVIDUAL.
Everything must make logical sense to me. I inherently need
to analyze, not so much to judge or identify with, but to ensure
things make sense according to my perspective. To draw a comparison, in mathematics, there are theorems in trigonometry. A
theorem is a statement that can be proved. If A, B, C, and D are
true, then E is a true statement. E is proven in each step by precise mathematical conditions. That is how my brain works. Of
course, when it comes to God, no matter how many "facts" are
laid out before us, there is inevitably some leap of faith involved.
Bottom line: When I said at the beginning of this book that I
spoke to God and that I'm not crazy, I meant it.

The most skeptical individual I had to convince about my
message from God was myself. For many years, I ran from
this experience, and I rarely ever shared it with another person. I didn't want anyone to think I was a kook or had turned
into some sort of religious zealot overnight. This is why my
search for the meaning of life, or my truth, was one of both
analytical study and spiritual exploration. I had gotten to a
point in my life where I needed answers for my questions. I

had experienced something incredible, but I felt that there had to be some meaning behind it. It couldn't have just been some random occurrence. That didn't make sense.

Part of what I decided to study along my journey of discovery was myself. If that was going to be fulfilling, I needed to find out things about myself from a logical perspective that would assist me in my quest to find out who I was, why I did the things I did, why I experienced the things I experienced—basically what made me tick and why. I am sharing some of this psychological information as best as I can.

> I needed to find out things about myself from a logical perspective that would assist me in my quest to find out who I was—basically what made me tick and why.

First, I wanted to learn how all human beings think and operate. I also wanted to know why I functioned as I did and why everyone else didn't always react in the same way. Freud's theories helped me understand so I could assimilate my spiritual experiences.

One of the biggest lessons I learned was about the ego and the effects it had on me and how I looked at life. I have also learned that the ego is something human beings have always had to deal with.

Egotism

The prime minister of the Tang Dynasty in China was a national hero for his success as both a statesman and a military leader. But despite his fame, power, and wealth, he considered himself a humble and devout Buddhist. Often he visited his favorite Zen master to study under him, and they seemed to get along very well. The fact that he was prime minister apparently had no effect on their relationship, which seemed to be simply one of a revered master and respectful student.

One day, during his usual visit, the prime minister asked the master, "Your Reverence, what is egotism according to Buddhism?" The master's face turned red, and in a very condescending and insulting tone of voice, he shot back, "What kind of stupid question is that?"

The unexpected response so shocked the prime minister that he became sullen and angry. The Zen master then smiled and said, "THIS, Your Excellency, is egotism."

The Zen master made his point about something that strongly affects our daily lives—*the ego.* It was famed psychiatrist Sigmund Freud who determined a great deal regarding what we know about the ego today. Freud proposed that the human personality is composed of three elements known as the *id*, the *ego*, and the *super ego.* These three components make us who we are, and they work together to create complex human behaviors. Consequently, our feelings, thoughts, and behaviors are the result of the interaction among *the id, the ego*, and *the super ego.* This interaction, however, leads to conflict, which creates anxiety, which leads to defense mechanisms that we create for ourselves. The key is to learn how to balance all three components to work in your favor. When we learn how to balance the three, we can shape our ego so it will not be so controlling. Shaping the ego, in conjunction with the three levels of mind from the previous chapter, allows us to see life in a totally different light. It allows us to find out who we truly are from a soul perspective.

The Base Personality

The *id* is the only component of the three that is present from birth. This part of the personality is entirely unconscious. It includes instinctive and primitive behaviors. Freud theorized that the id was the source of all psychic energy, which makes it the primary component of our personality.

The id strives for immediate gratification of all needs, wants, and desires. When not immediately met, mental tension or anxiety results. Since we are born with the id, it becomes an infant's way of expressing hunger or thirst, or feeling too hot, cold, or wet. The infant cries until its needs are satisfied.

Freud further theorized that the id tries to resolve tension through the primary processes, which involves forming a mental picture of the desired object to try to satisfy the perceived need. The energy for the id's action comes from libido and has two major instincts: *eros,* the life instinct that motivates people to focus on pleasure-seeking tendencies, and *thanatos,* the death instinct that motivates people to use aggressive urges to destroy.

Dealing with Reality

Unlike the id, the *ego* is the part of the personality that's aware of reality. It operates by recognizing what's real, and it understands that behaviors have consequences. The ego weighs the pros and cons of an action before it decides whether to act upon it.

During childhood, the ego develops perception, recognition, memory, and judgment using what Freud terms secondary processes. The ego, in other terms, acts as an arbitrator between the impulses of the id and the moralistic character of the super ego (described below). Because of its ability to reason and problem-solve, the ego is able to act as the buffer. It finds ways to satisfy the id's basic urges within the constraints of the super ego.

The Ethical Identity

The final personality aspect theorized by Freud is the *super ego.* This part of our personality contains our values and social morals. These attributes are typically learned in childhood and stored in our conscience. The super ego is the last part of the personality to develop, and it provides the guidelines of right and wrong for making judgments. Freud felt this part of our personality emerges around age five.

The super ego contains two parts. First is the *ego ideal*, which develops its own set of rules for behavioral standards. Second is the *conscience*, which stores all those situations deemed bad and taught to us as a child. The super ego acts to perfect and civilize our behavior according to learned experiences. It works to suppress the urges of the id. It also tries to make the ego act upon a perceived set of idealistic standards rather than upon more realistic principles.

Freud asserted that the key to a healthy personality is a balance between the id, the ego, and the super ego. If we allow the id to take control, impulses and self-gratification will take over our lives. Conversely, if we allow the super ego to take control, we are captive to rigid morals, and find ourselves becoming more and more judgmental and unbending in dealing with the outside world.

You have the opportunity to work on balancing these three, based not upon what you have been taught by others, but by realizing what your self-beliefs are. The good news is that you are not helpless. With some soul-searching and self-analysis, you will craft blueprints detailed enough to allow yourself to build the life you desire.

Pitfalls of the Ego

All the turmoil between the id, ego, and super ego makes it difficult to effectively manage the pressures within, unless you have good ego strength. Though it may sometimes feel like walking on a high wire, maintaining good ego strength is essential in order to rise to our highest good. The ego, however, is not necessarily our best friend.

Though I didn't realize it at the time, I learned a lot about ego while at the Magee Rehab Hospital. Before Magee, I had made a bargain with God to get what I wanted (the ability to walk). From an egoist standpoint, being left in a wheelchair would not leave me a whole person, based on my view of the world, and I felt I would become a lesser individual. Even before the accident, I had allowed ego to drive my life. I separated from God and the church, determined to rely only on myself, and became quite successful in the process. At Magee, I had little control over my body, and my future was unknown. However, I did have control over what I saw. My observations, if I just allowed the ego to take over, would quickly turn into judgments.

Egos are important parts of personalities, but we cannot let them run our lives. Too often we do things in a fight-or-flight response caused by our ego's perception of the outside world. If we had looked at a situation differently, a more beneficial outcome might have occurred.

Webster defines ego as "the self as distinct from the external one." It is the division of the psyche that is conscious and most immediately controls behavior. It is the part of us most in touch with external reality. It creates the illusion that we are separate from others and from God. Freud defined the ego as "the representative of the outer world to the id," with id being the libido or inner feeling self. While the id gravitates toward internal instincts, the ego separates itself by anchoring perceptions in the real world. The ego does not feel. It thinks, analyzes, and blames.

The ego is constantly thinking, observing, and judging. Perhaps you just read that last statement and heard the voice in your head say something along the lines of "That's stupid!" That was your ego. It throws up barriers and blames others for everything to provide an illusion of safety within our thought patterns. These thought patterns are based upon the belief systems we have created for ourselves since childhood.

My Beginning

We all have, I suppose, lessons to learn while on this earth, and I am no different. I came from a childhood of dysfunction. I'm not seeking sympathy. In fact, I'm trying to keep ego out as I write this. You know, whatever your "story" is, it's generally developed by your ego. But these issues were a deep wound within me as far back as I can remember. My father was a functional alcoholic. He was extremely hard working, but after work his intake of alcohol seemed to never stop. My mother was an enabler. She constantly complained about the situation but never did anything about it and usually assisted in the madness. My brothers and I were the ones who took the brunt of the misery.

I am the man I am today because of my parents and in spite of them.

This is a classic recipe for dysfunction, and I lived it and survived it. I am the man I am today because of my parents and in spite of them. Despite his shortcomings, my father taught me much. The positive traits built by my childhood include a good work ethic, helping others out without expecting anything in return, and continuing to move forward despite the clouds of disaster that may lie ahead. Beneath it all, my father was a good man, yet once the alcohol started flowing, he turned from a Dr. Jekyll into a Mr. Hyde.

The emotional strain bordered on unbearable from my earliest memories. While my parents screamed at each other, I lay in bed begging God to put a stop to it—always to no avail. I would be so scared and upset during these episodes that I had difficulty breathing. My father didn't allow my mother to work, so my formative years were spent with her. As I've mentioned, she was a woman who lived her entire life in fear of absolutely everything. I picked up on this vibe at an early age and became a fearful child. I was so introverted because of this dysfunction that I acted extremely shy in childhood.

Among all the turmoil in our household, I had three younger brothers who I felt I had to protect. There were many times when I felt as if I needed to act as a parent. That's a lot of pressure to put on a kid, especially when, at an early age, your mother tells you she wished you were never born. I often felt unloved and alone, and I knew my brothers felt the same way. I believed that, one way or another, we had to stick together and find our own way in the world. I couldn't depend on these two adults—who weren't even able to save themselves—to protect us. It became my job to keep my brothers and myself safe.

I can honestly say that I never heard my dad once tell me that he loved me. Yet, in some weird, wacky way, I know that he did. I strove always to make him proud of me; I was certain at that moment he would tell me how much he did love me. That moment never came. No wonder I developed worthiness issues. Nothing was ever good enough. I had become, and still am to a certain extent, a perfectionist. I also was my own worst enemy. Everything had a condition to it. Growing up in that environment was extremely difficult and confusing. I saw how the other kids interacted with their parents and thought there must be something wrong with me. I had to find the key to winning my parents' approval. As I look back on those times, I think it was more of surviving than growing through childhood. In the world I knew at that time, the Lack-of-Self-Esteem Boat was loaded and setting sail.

Later I began to realize that the world-at-large was not as black-and-white as my home environment. By that, I mean everything there was always an absolute; either/or, yes/no—there were no possibilities for an alternate answer. Little by little, I began to see a whole lot of gray. As I got out of the environment I was raised in, it was as if a light had been shined on me. I recognized different opportunities. I started to learn that I didn't have to go to one of the black or white extremes. I had new input on the direction my life could go in. Additionally, I realized that getting ahead depended on how you used those shades of gray to your advantage. Even with this knowledge firmly in hand, the ego continuously took control. Then I judged every situation I was in, whether personal or business, as either good or bad. If judged bad, then I was done and it was time to move on. It was time to find someone else who would love me based on what I perceived to be my needs, or to proceed on to things I thought were going to give me pleasure and make the pain inside stop.

The ego can protect us and keep us from harm, but it doesn't need to dictate every experience we have.

Controlling the Ego

Only in the years subsequent to the accident have I gone deep within to find answers. One of the biggest answers I have found is to minimize the ego. Yes, the ego can protect us and keep us from harm, but it doesn't need to dictate every experience we have. As I learned to love and let go, without having any preconceived judgments as to whether something was good or bad, the Universe (God) opened up and poured out its blessings in all my experiences. I look at things very differently today. And keeping the judgment turned off allows me to experience every situation for what it is.

Every experience we have is recorded in our mind. Whatever the experience, it is observed by the ego, thought about by the ego, and judged by the ego to be good or bad. We can certainly work to overcome our fears, but in order to do that, we must learn to diffuse the ego. Very, very few people have ever been able to eliminate it. I have learned that working on just trying to control the ego can provide extremely beneficial results. The ego does, however, serve a purpose. It's important in thinking problems through and observing behavior. For this reason, we need to develop a dual approach in any situation. For example, we need to consider how something makes us feel, as well as tapping into the thought process of the mind. The key here is learning how to use the mind as a tool, rather than letting our mind use *us* as a tool.

The ego's ultimate fear is death. According to Buddhism, the concept of life and death is merely a delusional way of thinking that is dualistic. The denial of being dead one day is how the ego affirms itself as being alive now. To be self-conscious is to be conscious of one's self, to hold onto the notion of being alive. Buddhists claim that the ego-self is not a thing, not what we really are, but is instead a mental construction. Anxiety is generated by identifying with this fiction, for the simple reason that we don't know and can't know what this thing that we supposedly are actually is. This is why the shadow of the sense of self will inevitably be a sense of lack.

A Course in Miracles defines the ego as the wish to be separate from God. The ego is the denial of God as our Creator and an attempt to make ourselves our own creator. As such, the ego is delusional. We created the ego to make a world for us in which we are special and separate from each other. During my recovery, I bargained with God, and then when he had fulfilled his promise, I called on Him for help but "took over" as soon as plans were moving forward again. I had that "I can take it from here" mindset. At the very moment I called on God and He answered, I separated in "independence."

With this behavior, it's no wonder that we often get the feeling that something is lacking in life. The ego has a deep-seated fear of such incompleteness. It manifests itself in the form of "being worthy" or "good enough." As I have stated previously, I've always been a perfectionist. This inner demon drove me to prove myself to the outside world when it was never necessary. Even if one thing ended up slightly flawed despite another 20 turning out perfectly, I obsessed and beat myself up over the one mistake. I was never good enough as far as I (my ego) was concerned. Many others have had this same thought process, at least in my opinion. Many of us also strive for possessions, money, success, or power to try to fill this inner black hole. We hope it will make us feel better, but it usually doesn't work. Once we attain what we are seeking, we soon realize that the hole within us is still there.

Emptiness and the Ego

A mere six years after my accident, after losing everything I had and then working to get it all back, I sat in the family room of my dream home completed only five months earlier. I thought this house was going to do it for me. I thought it completed the climb from rock bottom back to the top. But it didn't. I remember sitting there, a fire blazing in the fireplace, thinking, *This will not do it. So what am I going to do next?*

That was the story of my adult life—this vicious circle of trying to attain perfection, only to achieve something and soon realize the hole within still existed. It was a slow process after my accident, but time allowed me to start looking at life in a different way.

I know I spent many years with my ego in the driver's seat. I always focused on becoming something or trying to achieve something. It was due to my ego. In my mind, I was never good enough. So every time I reached a goal or attained something, my ego told me I wasn't worthy of it. The misery perpetuated. Even in my relationships, I often looked for a woman to give meaning to my life. It was only a matter of time (usually not very long) before I was disillusioned and on to the next conquest.

What a sneaky thing this ego can be—we don't realize the damage it can cause.

From birth, we watch others and begin to develop as an individual. We start to feel and develop a sense of self, or separateness, and this separateness needs to identify with external things. Early on, the ego also discovers the need to defend itself. It's important to understand, however, that we don't need to identify with this. We are all connected as one in the Universe. The more we realize this, the more we begin to see how much the Universe (God) works in conjunction with us to supply our needs and desires.

Another thing the ego does is develop the concept that we are either better than others or not as good. As far as the ego is concerned, we are either a success or a failure. What a sneaky thing this ego can be—and because it develops at such an early age, we don't realize the damage it can cause.

Many times after my accident, while in the hospital, I would sit in my wheelchair and wonder how I could go on because I was not, at least according to my ego, a whole person. Now I never had this experience before, so how could I know whether I was a whole person? The answer came from my ego, simply from the preconceived judgments it had developed. The ego prevents us from seeing the world as whole by labeling and judging everything it sees. Yet the Bible provides instruction. Matthew 7:1-2 (NRSV) states, "Do not judge, or you too will be judged. For in the same way you judge others, you will be judged, and with the measure you use, it will be measured to you."

Good Ego

As much as I write about how bad the ego is, I do need to note once again that the ego does serve a purpose. The ego helps us to remain focused and to achieve a balance between what is ethical and what our primal desires are. The ego gives us the ability to change, the ability to remain flexible, and the ability to maintain confidence. We learn to move away from the ego-centered pride and the need to compete by becoming conscious of the ego and what it brings to the table—desires, distractions, fears, and compulsions.

By working on taming the ego and allowing the id (feeling) to become part of the decision-making process, we begin to see things more clearly and without preconceived notions thrown out by the ego. Rather than think of ourselves as superior to others, we should look within ourselves to clearly determine the path we are to follow. Matthew 7:3-5 says, "Why do you look at the speck of sawdust in your brother's eye and pay no attention to the plank in your own eye? How can you say to your brother, 'Let me take the speck out of your eye,' when all the time there is a plank in your own eye? You hypocrite, first take the plank out of your own eye, and then you will see clearly to remove the speck from your brother's eye."

As I look back on my life, I see opportunities missed perhaps due to my ego attempting to control it all. Today, I don't do that. I am much more reasoned and much less judgmental. This allows me a clarity I never chose to experience before. It helps me make better choices for true success, rather than success determined by what the ego thinks. Don't get me wrong. I haven't completely eliminated the ego. I simply try to do my best to keep the ego in balance with the other parts of my personality. At times, I still must grapple the steering wheel from ego's control.

Minimizing the Ego

I know how hard it can be to minimize the ego. My moment of enlightenment (yes, pun intended) was in the rehabilitation hospital after the accident. Each morning after breakfast and before physical therapy, we had the opportunity to go outside on the second floor sundeck. Most people went out to smoke. I went out to get sun on my face. I love being outdoors in the summer.

This deck overlooked Race Street in Philadelphia, which was a secondary eastbound artery out of Center City heading toward the bridges of New Jersey. Oh, how I longed to be on Race Street! Early on, I would watch rush-hour traffic below and seethe with anger that I was stuck in a wheelchair watching life from the sidelines. *How could they get along without me?* I wondered. I couldn't understand.

As time went on, I noticed that in looking slightly to the right I saw the most incredible view of the skyline of the city, which was only a 5- to 10-minute walk from where I was stuck. As I focused on the skyline, I noticed that every few days, at the top of the Liberty Towers (the two tallest buildings in Philadelphia at that time), a hatch opened from the pointed glass-enclosed top, and a man wearing a harness popped out to do something atop the building. He appeared to be, from my vantage point, the size of an ant. It was at that point when I slowly began to surrender to the now and realize how infinitesimally small we all are. Yes, people would miss me if I wasn't here any longer, but the world and life would continue on without skipping a beat. Not until this realization could I begin to appreciate my smallness within the greater whole. And the ego began to shrink.

What a monster the ego can be! Assuming your ego has not caused you to slam the book shut and shout, "This is ridiculous," I'd like to share work we can do to minimize the ego. These are suggestions learned mostly through my accident and recovery.

Meditation: The practice of meditation has been a huge help for me, and controlling the ego simply came as a by-product. Meditation is the art of concentration and being able to quiet the mind. (I discuss it further in Chapter 13, "Why Not Create Your Reality?") Practicing the concept of oneness has allowed me to overcome feelings of fear, isolation, and individuality. I know my mind is often going a thousand miles a minute with competing thoughts, but when I can sit, get quiet, and focus on the inner silence, I know I'm not by myself in the world.

There are many ways to meditate. Its most basic form entails finding a quiet space within. This sometimes naturally occurs when you're enjoying nature while camping, hiking, or spending time at the beach. As you tune in to the beauty of your surroundings, thoughts quiet and the beauty and breathing are all that's left. Beginners are sometimes taught to achieve this feeling anywhere by concentrating on inhaling and exhaling. Consciously slowing each breath forces the mind to clear. Take "belly breaths." These are the deep, full breaths we naturally take as infants and during childhood. The belly should expand (rather than the shoulders rising during the inhale). When your mind begins interrupting with noise of daily tasks, count each breath until your mind is still again.

I constantly strive to find ways to meditate that work well for me. You, too, should find a method that's comfortable and relaxing. Plenty of information exists to help you get started.

It may not be easy (it wasn't for me), but the benefits are extraordinary—especially at times when you really feel you're in need of a miracle. Try it! Then continue to work at it until going into a meditative state becomes second nature.

Strong Self-Esteem: This is a hot button for me. Many, many years of feeling inadequate never allowed me to be who I am. I always tried to be what other people wanted me to be in order to feel worthy. Now, if this was never an issue for you, you may not be able to understand what I'm saying. However, if you've struggled with this, I know it resonates as if I'm preaching to the choir.

You are a divine being right as you are at this moment. No one has ever experienced the world or ever will through your eyes.

You are a divine being right as you are at this moment. You are the power and presence of God. No one has ever experienced the world or ever will through your eyes. Your existence is a point of God expressing Himself right here and right now. What a cool fact! There is only one you. Knowing and believing this allows us to develop a healthy self-esteem. And a healthy self-esteem develops a healthy ego.

What does this mean? A person free of insecurities or with few self-doubts provides the ego no ammunition to use when life presents a challenge. The healthy ego will not react negatively to defend itself, or rationalize itself when faced with a challenge; it knows that whatever is going on outside has no effect with who the person is on the inside. It is what I like to call "being okay with ourselves." How can we accomplish this? Start by refining your inner self-talk to be positive, calming, and self-loving. Then reactivity doesn't become an option.

Overcome Fears: The best way to do this is to do something you fear. The ego has established every fear you have. Many are not justifiable. Step outside your comfort zone and

do something you fear. Soon you'll soon realize how inconsequential the fear was to begin with. Again, the primary
example in my life came completely by accident (no pun intended). I think the major turning point was when I had my
near-death experience. Earlier, I described it
as not so much watching my life pass before
my eyes but a moment of acceptance when
I wouldn't fear death, pain, or suffering anymore. Something within that experience had
a profound effect on me and changed the direction of my life. Although situations come
up from time to time that evoke some level of
fear within me, they don't stop me in my tracks as they did
earlier. Besides, when comparing them to dying, they have
absolutely no control over me.

Step outside your comfort zone and do something you fear. Soon you'll soon realize how inconsequential the fear was to begin with.

Now I grant you that my experience with death allows
me to look at whatever I'm facing and realize that there's no
comparison to dying and therefore nothing to fear. I know
this is a rather extreme example to give, but there are other
less extreme things at our disposal. Fear of flying. Intimacy.
I could go on and on. The good news? These fears melt away
when we learn with each one that we have the power and the
ability to step past them.

Keeping the inner self-talk positive is important in facing
fears. Try to catch yourself when your talk gets negative when
you're fearful. What's the basis for your fear? What negative
thought(s) are in your head? Take some deep breaths and analyze
what's at the core of your fear. Once you detach from the emotion, it's usually much easier to see that what we fear has no basis
to begin with. Look at the issue and then respond with positive
statements to counter the negative thoughts in your head. You
will ultimately see that it never was as bad as you thought.

Step Out of the Norm: Everyone struggles with this to some degree. It's human nature to settle into routines. Some routines are short-lived. Some last a lifetime. As we continue with the routine, the ego judges it as safe. Sometimes we need to break out of our routines to get our life moving in a different direction. It's a great exercise for self-discipline.

How to Start Doing Things Differently

Begin by trying options that you wouldn't typically choose. This could be as simple as choosing a new food, taking a different route to work, or wearing a brighter-colored shirt than normal. Note how good it feels. Next, move up to bigger changes or riskier things until eventually you journey way outside your boundaries. You will feel more confident and stronger than you ever have. It can be invigorating and is the first step toward breaking old patterns. If you find it difficult, begin on a smaller scale. Commit to doing something different once each week.

The sitcom *Seinfeld* had a great episode in which George Costanza was in the coffee shop complaining about his life as he ordered what he always orders. Jerry mockingly suggests that if he orders the same meal all the time and is getting the same results, why not order the exact opposite? George gets inspired, does exactly that, and for at least for one episode, his life changes in fabulous ways. He meets an attractive woman in the coffee shop. She eventually gets him an interview with her uncle, who works for the New York Yankees. George gets the job, which had been a dream of his since childhood. He took a step outside the norm.

Any change in your thought process will help you grow. Allow the ego to understand that there's always more than one option. You will reach a point where you embrace change and the growth it uncovers.

Stepping outside the norm is choosing to bring change to your life. Sometimes, though, change is inevitable. When we're already making changes and find that they enrich our lives, the changes forced upon us become easier to handle.

As you work on your ego, you'll find that other tests will show up from time to time that allow you to refine your ability to see situations from a variety of perspectives. It's not all about the ego. As much as the ego serves a purpose, it limits your ability to be the shining light you are. It may not be possible to totally eliminate the ego, but it's your choice at all times to either respond or react to any given situation. Responding utilizes the free will which God has given all of us. Since He has given us free will, why not put it to good use? Responding allows you to analyze the situation, look at alternatives, and make the best possible choice. Merely reacting to a situation limits your possibilities and potential outcomes.

Chapter 8

The Universal Laws

METAPHYSICS IS THE STUDY OF THE LAWS that govern the Universe. Learning how to live in harmony with these principles determines our successes on our journey from birth to death.

Meanwhile, Nature is a continual ebb and flow that constitutes life. We see seasonal changes each year. The harvest reflects the cycle of life. The rising and setting of the sun demarks the days. The moon waxes and wanes throughout each month. It seems that when we are in rhythm with these cycles and phases, we are in rhythm with creation. We are "in the flow."

Universal energy exists all around us and moves within us. The energy that provides us life is the same energy that runs the Universe. These patterns and rhythms of energy imply an intelligence, a Creator, or what many call God. The ways these patterns of energy move have been described within Universal Laws. When we understand these Laws, we have the opportunity to connect with our Creator and exist in the flow.

Living in the flow allows you to become balanced. Balance allows you to live life effortlessly and to manifest your dreams and desires by being in sync with life. Once we realize that everything operates under Universal or Natural Laws, we see and begin to understand that the Universe operates in perfect order. Throw in God-given free will, and we have the choice to work within these Laws or to work against them. As with anything else, it's much easier and more fulfilling to work *with* something than to work against it.

Partial List of Universal Laws

The Law of Allowing
The Law of Attraction
The Law of Belief
The Law of Cause and Effect (Karma)
The Law of Control
The Law of Detachment
The Law of Expectations
The Law of Gratitude
The Law of Intentional Creation (Deliberate Creation)
The Law of Love
The Law of Polarity
The Law of Pure Potentiality
The Law of Sufficiency and Abundance
The Law of Thought

Universal Laws apply to everyone equally. We don't need to understand all the nuances of the Law of Gravity, for instance, but jump off a building and you are going to feel the effect of it. These Laws are evidence of unseen power in the Universe. Depending on how we feel about something, the Universal Laws can act in a positive or negative way. We are responsible for the results of our beliefs, thoughts, and actions. The good news is that when we think positively in conjunction with the Universal Laws, we see progress in our lives.

It's difficult to verify how many Universal Laws exist. Several overlap, so there is no consensus. The boxed list shows some of the Universal Laws that I have read about and/or studied. They are the ones that have had a significant impact on my life. I discuss them below.

The Law of Attraction

Although the Laws are presented in no particular order, the *Law of Attraction* must go first, as I feel it's the most important. It is likely the most well-known Universal Law. This Law has become the "get what you want by thinking the right thought" hit of the decade. Books, movies, and seminars all preach the wonderful results of this Law and how you can use it to get whatever it is you want. But can you? *Yes—but with some caveats.*

Simply put, the Law of Attraction states that we attract whatever we put our attention on. The Universe is pure vibratory energy and so are our thoughts. The thoughts we focus on match up, or align, with similar energy vibrations in the Universe, which then appear in our reality. In essence, we attract the experiences we focus our thoughts on.

Many of our thought patterns are based on childhood experiences, and many realities continue to appear due to these ingrained thought processes. We can change our results by changing our thoughts. This is very simple, yet very difficult for many people to do. We really can achieve a different result simply by thinking differently about something. When I say think differently about something, I really mean think about it being true deep down in your core. This is what happened when I was the only one who truly believed I would walk again. I believed deep within my core. It takes focus, commitment, and practice.

Keep in mind that the Universe doesn't differentiate between positive thought patterns or negative thought patterns. It wants to provide for you, and it will—either way. What you think about is what the Universe assumes you want; it makes no judgments about it—if you want it, you get it. No good, no bad, just creation. This Law has been taught by humankind since Biblical times. The Law also ties into the Law of Cause and Effect, also known as *Karma*.

The Law of Cause and Effect (Karma)

This Law demonstrates that we are active participants in life. Our will has effect. When the Law of Cause and Effect is understood, amazing possibilities begin to occur. The link between thoughts, words, and actions and what develops in reality becomes apparent. What we put into the Universe, whether it is positive or negative, is what we get back. No judgments, no excuses.

What we put into the Universe, whether it is positive or negative, is what we get back.

If you put it out there, be certain it's what you want to come back, because it will. My second chance at life is an example. I believed the voice answering my prayer, and I took action to help it come true. I also encouraged those around me to believe that miracles can happen.

The Law of Cause and Effect confirms that you are, in fact, a co-creator of your experience. You are not here by happenstance. Once you understand this concept, believe this concept, and see the effects of this concept, your life will change. This Law, in conjunction with The Law of Attraction, allows you to create the life you really want.

The Law of Allowing

The *Law of Allowing* simply refers to dropping all judgments and emotional attachments to others—who they are, what they have, and what they do. If we judge someone or something, that produces negative vibrations, and as a result, that negativity continues to be our reality. It doesn't mean that we allow others to do whatever they want to us without repercussions (see the last law, Karma). However, it doesn't do us any good to judge it. Simply allow things to be as they are. Life is what it is. Applying this Law to your life will bring you freedom. Focus on yourself and don't worry about others. Life (and our experience of it) is too short.

The Law of Love

Love is energy. Love is all there is. Love is also acknowledging that all things are one. We are all connected, part of a single universal energy. This Law will ensure that you see this truth.

You cannot leave an experience permanently until you exit with love and acceptance. Otherwise, the same experience will continue to appear in your reality. I remember a few years ago, I got into a bad business deal that lasted less than one year. However, because of my desire for revenge, or at least what I envisioned as my Karma, this situation dragged on for another full year. It cost me a lot of money, but more importantly, it brought an end to a five-year relationship with my girlfriend because I had let the situation consume me.

My whole life was on hold because of my anger, and the need for retaliation had taken hold of me. Once I started to accept the situation with love, this experience began to disappear from my reality. Now accepting it doesn't mean that I thought it was okay for them to do what they did—*not at all.* But I had entered into the agreement willingly and took full responsibility for my part. Nobody had forced me to get involved. Note that acceptance doesn't mean giving up. On the contrary, accepting something for what it is allows us to move forward and change, if we want. Or we can sit and wallow in our misery.

The great thing about this Law is that once it starts to take hold because you're on board with it, things do begin to happen. My ex-business partners had an office down the street from my newly created job experience. Every day I passed it on my way to work. I think perhaps the Universe was allowing me to get a full dose to get it all out of my system. In any event, as I began to accept it for what it was (just an experience), it didn't bother me coming to work each day. As time passed, because of bad business decisions, they closed their office. Ultimately, my new company took over a construction project that my former business partners had defaulted on, which had been taken back by the bank.

The Law of Thought

We create our reality with our thoughts. Whatever we focus our thoughts on becomes our reality in some way, shape,

> *We create our reality with our thoughts. Whatever we focus our thoughts on becomes our reality in some way, shape, or form.*

or form. Our thoughts develop from our attitudes and beliefs. These have been programmed into our subconscious mind. This is why it's hard at first to change a thought. The subconscious mind is much more powerful than the conscious mind. With practice, and forgiving ourselves when we stumble, we can change that programming. Our thoughts can then create a more positive reality. What we believe will happen.

The Law of Intentional Creation (Deliberate Creation)

We create all of our personal experiences. Whereas the Law of Attraction brings us reality based on our energy vibrations, the *Law of Intentional Creation* is a vibration specifically put out to the Universe. The Law of Attraction responds and provides, even when we unknowingly put out vibrations. Intentional Creation occurs when we specifically concentrate on what we want in life and ask that it be brought to us.

The Law of Gratitude

An attitude of gratitude will assist your manifestations immensely. Why? Because gratitude completes the cycle of knowing by thanking the Universe for what it has provided. Whatever you are grateful for is what the Universe wants to continue giving to you. Having a grateful attitude allows positives to manifest and negatives to fade away. As simple as this may sound, it carries great importance.

The Law of Detachment

The *Law of Detachment* states that in order to acquire anything, you must relinquish your attachment to it. This is all about trust. The more you learn to trust, the more of a deliberate co-creator you become. Remember, every time Jesus prayed, he thanked God in advance and never questioned the result. By detaching from it, the truth becomes reality. Put your thought (vision) out there and then let the Law of Allowing take over.

We often slow our desires from coming to fruition simply because we stand in the way of the Universe.

We often slow our desires from coming to fruition simply because we stand in the way of the Universe. This happens when we don't trust ourselves. We often think the Universe doesn't know exactly what we want, and so we try to micromanage the process. The truth is, most often the Universe has the best plan and we try to steer it toward something far less. Our distrust ends up getting in the way.

The Law of Sufficiency and Abundance

This Law states that we have everything within each of us right now to create anything we want. Every option, every possibility, is at our disposal. There is abundance in the Universe—enough of everything for everyone. There are no shortages. We are complete and whole as we currently are. We don't lack anything.

The Law of Polarity

Simply stated, this Law pronounces that Unity is plural at a minimum of two. What does this mean? Well, the *Law of Polarity* is the ability to understand transformation. You can choose to shift your perception from bad to good. Once you accomplish that simple task, your reality changes. This Law also works in conjunction with the Law of Cause and Effect. It's entirely up to you how to view a situation. Good or bad, however you view it determines your reality.

The Law of Pure Potentiality

This Law states that the true essence of who we are is pure consciousness. It is Source (God, Universe) seeking to express itself into form through us. God is within us, not separate from us. We must realize that we are in alignment with the Power that manifests everything in the world. Therefore, anything is possible. The only limits to our creativity are the limits we put on ourselves.

The Law of Control

This Law states that you feel positive about yourself to the degree that you're in control of your life. Conversely, you feel negative about yourself to the degree that you're not in control. This is recognized in psychology as "locus of control." ("Locus" means the location or center where something is situated or occurs.) It's generally agreed that most stress, anxiety, tension, and

Control over your life begins with your thoughts, and thoughts are the only thing you have complete control over!

psychosomatic illnesses occur as a result of a person feeling out of control.

You can have either internal or external locus of control. Feeling confident, happy, and in charge of your life are internal, while feeling like a victim, helpless, trapped, or controlled by others are external. In every case, control over your life begins with your thoughts, and thoughts are the only thing you have complete control over!

The Law of Belief

The *Law of Belief* states that whatever you believe, with feeling, becomes your reality. The more intensely you believe something to be true for you, the faster it comes to you. Think of a thought as a nail and the emotion behind it as a hammer driving it home. With concentration and enough force, you can set the nail in one or two blows. The Law of Belief requires intense focus, like tunnel vision, filtering out information that is not consistent with the belief. William James said, "Belief creates the actual fact." The Bible says, "According to your faith (belief), it is done unto you." What you believe, you will have.

The benevolent worldview would be a nice place to live, helpful people, abundance, and so on, and the world conspires. Conversely, the malevolent worldview would be the rich get richer, the poor get poorer, you can't fight city hall, and so on, and the world conspires. Self-limiting beliefs hold you back. For example, you may not believe in your ability to learn or remember because you didn't do well in high school or may not have gone on to college, and so you are limited. What you believe with emotion and conviction, even if false, will become your reality.

This doesn't mean what you believe is true. It just means that your own perception of it is your personal reality. Most self-limiting beliefs are not true. They are based on negative information that we have taken in and accepted as true for us. Henry Ford said, "Whether we think we can or think we can't—we are right." Identify your self-limiting beliefs. They can be changed.

The Law of Expectations

This Law states that whatever you expect in confidence becomes your self-fulfilling prophecy. How many times do we sabotage ourselves with our thoughts? Successful men and women who expect to be liked and happy are seldom disappointed. So are the ones who are pessimistic and cynical. They are never let down either.

Expectations take different forms. Some are internal (coming from us) and others are external (coming from other people). The four main forms are:

1. **Your parents:** We are programmed to try to live up to, or down to, our parents' expectations, sometimes many years after they are gone. I once read that many prisoners interviewed by psychologists reported that they had been told over and over again that someday they would end up in prison.

2. **Your boss and your performance:** If a boss has positive expectations of his employees, they tend to be happier, more productive people.

3. **Child expectations:** Confidently and constantly expect the very best from your children. They will not try to disappoint you, and you will not be disappointed.

4. **Yourself:** Your expectations of yourself can override the most negative expectations that anyone else may have of you. W. Clement Stone, multi-millionaire insurance fel-

low and author, was inverse paranoid. He believed that everyone and every situation was conspiring to show him a benefit or teach him some valuable lesson. Say to yourself, "Something wonderful is going to happen to me today." Try it for a few weeks and see what happens. You will be surprised!

What's Holding You Back?

Do you see how clearly these Laws work? Although a few may seem similar, there are little nuances in each. When we follow these Laws, we are in flow with them and with the Universe (God). Life becomes so effortless and prosperous. Or you can continue swimming against the current like a salmon until you are worn out. Resisting these Laws will only waste time and slow you from achieving your goals and desires.

With all these Laws working for us, what seems to be holding us back? Many possible factors, including:

- **A lack of self-worth:** This says I'm not worthy of having anything good in my life. I'm a loser and meant to struggle.
- **A lack of understanding:** You know these Laws exist but don't understand how the manifestation process can work for you.
- **Not trusting in yourself:** Remember, distrust blocks the Universe from acting and manifesting our desires.
- **A lack of commitment on your part:** The funny thing is that it doesn't even take that much commitment to start with.
- **Demanding a specific timeframe:** This can prevent things from manifesting.
- **Playing the part of the victim:** The victim sets conditions. Before I can get what I want, something (or someone) must change.

There hasn't been a time in our lives when we have not had one or more of these issues. I'll admit that I have had most of them, and many at the same time! However, the more I have gone within to heal myself, the more these stumbling blocks diminished. Once in a while, something may trigger a reaction from an event in my past, and I need to get hold of myself and realize who I am: *a co-creating spiritual being here to experience the wonders of this life.* I am not here to sit and suffer.

All the Laws described in this chapter are simple laws. There's no need for long expansive periods of study. They are easy to grasp, and the more you consider them and apply them, the easier manifestation becomes. Your desires await you. There is no right and wrong here. Like I pointed out earlier, all these Laws continuously function just as the Law of Gravity does. I may not be able to totally understand the nuances of the Law of Gravity, but jump, fall, or get pushed from a height—the result is all the same!

The Universal Laws function whether or not you want them to and whether or not you even know they exist. You have two choices. You can apply these Laws by accident, by chance, or by ignorance and get spotty results. Or you can apply these Laws consciously and await the beauty and splendor you always dreamed possible.

Chapter 9

Be Still

WE ALL HAVE THE INHERENT ABILITY TO CREATE our reality. I have discussed some of the Universal Laws that are involved. One of the trickier parts is understanding exactly how to make it happen. Do we stand back and wait for the skies to part? Or do we immediately begin to jam the square peg in the round hole? Perhaps the answer lies somewhere in between. There's something to be said for stillness.

When I had that moment of connection with God (the Universe) in the hospital room late one night, I knew I would be healed no matter what anyone had said, was saying, or would say about my situation. The key to it all is to be still and watch what the Universe does to create.

Assisting the Universe

You have work to do, so it's important to watch for signs to assist the Universe. You're not the director, and it won't occur when you want it. It's a collaboration that happens for each and every one of us if we're willing to do what's required. Lately there has been a big run on creating our realities from purely a materialistic point of view. This is fine, but you'll find that creation from that standpoint is far less fulfilling than what you can do when you approach creation from other views.

Other ways to create your reality include a reality of peace, a reality of love, and a reality of healing. These are more important, in my opinion, than anything we can achieve from a materialistic perspective. Don't get me wrong, I like prosperity. In fact, I love prosperity, but I also love to be at peace with myself. That's one of the most important things I have come to appreciate.

You can, however, create the materialistic and the deeper realities together. In fact, the materialistic will stay with you longer when it has been created with love and a deeper vision of spirituality. When you ask for money from the reality of love, and also express the desire to create things with love, healing, and peace, you may find that your business or career takes on new meaning. You may gain new clients, a job offer, or get a promotion. You will get more money, but you will also have more of the love, healing, and peace that you have asked for as well. You will be much more satisfied and find that you really love what you're doing, do a better job, and get more money all at the same time.

I first really began to take notice of this "phenomenon" while I was at Magee rehabilitating. Prior to the accident, I was such a control freak that I really believed it was up to me to make things happen. If I wanted something, I wouldn't accept "No" for an answer. I was continually jamming the square peg into the round hole, whether it wanted to fit or not. And many times, there was dissatisfaction on my part with the results I got. Usually, it wound up being something I didn't really want to begin with. But at Magee, I was physically incapable of forcing what I wanted to happen. I couldn't leave my surroundings either. I was stuck there having to deal with myself stripped of all outside influences that might have had an effect on my choices. I had no choice but to get still, surrender, and continue to be in the unknown.

Surrender doesn't imply giving up and accepting what is. Surrender is the point of allowing a quietness to occur in which answers appear. Many times, we don't see or hear these answers because we're too busy trying to force an outcome. It was at one of the lowest points in my life when I began to witness amazing occurrences by being still and paying attention. There are times today when I get caught up in the frenzy of life and miss out on answers I'm waiting for. I just have to remember to shut up and listen.

Waiting for Our Intentions

One of the greatest lines in the Bible is in Psalm 46: "Be still, and know that I am God." When we put any intention out to the Universe, we need to state it, believe it, and be patient while the Universe delivers it. What we are asking for has already been created (at the moment of our request), so we must allow the Universe to bring it into our reality. If we dwell on it not coming to pass, that is what will show up.

The more I practice this, the more I am learning to trust my intuition. Not some thought that pops into my head telling me that I should do something, but rather an inner knowing that I should do something. When I do it, I know it is my intuition because I am at peace. You don't know whether opportunities, situations, places, or people will be drawn in to assist you, but be ready to act on whatever occurs. This is a co-creative experience. You're not separate, and you're not alone.

Suppose, for example, you want to plant carrots in your garden. You cannot plant the seeds and sit back and do noth-

Mixing Stillness & Action

Be still. This doesn't mean do nothing; instead, be ready to act when an inspired idea strikes you. Be ready when someone shows up out of nowhere to assist you along your way. Be ready for whatever occurs at any given moment that you know is assisting you.

Sure, it's easier to focus on the difficulties, to continually list grievances about your current situation. Try something different. *State what you want.* Focus on what you want. Get still and listen.

This doesn't imply inaction. On the contrary, being in stillness, knowing that the Universe is working for you, is the opposite of inaction. It is the action that's needed. If you put forth an intention but just sit still waiting for something to appear or change, you are a dreamer. Again, we don't want to force things to happen, but rather be in the trusting stillness within and *watch for opportunities to do your part.* Sometimes action is required that will take you out of your comfort zone. Remember, the Universe is with you step-by-step and will assist you in your every need.

ing. The carrots will not grow. If you plant the seeds and do what is required on your part—water the seeds, weed the garden, and fertilize the plants—the carrots will grow. However, if you get impatient and go out to the garden after only one week and dig up the garden to see if you have carrots, you will be disappointed. You have to allow the Universe to do its thing.

Jesus said, "So I tell you, whatever you ask for in prayer, believe you have received it, and it will be yours." (Mark 11:24) However simplistic that statement may sound, it's actually extremely profound. Ask, believe, and receive. If you're not in alignment and put out confusing signals to the Universe, the Universe cannot respond. If you focus on having, the Universe will provide. If you focus on not having, the Universe will also provide.

A Level of Trust

There's another way to achieve our desires. I call it "a level of trust." (I've also seen the term "trustful passivity" used in writing published almost a century ago.) In other words, there are things we need to do, but there are things we need to allow the Universe to do without us getting involved and fouling up the works. This is accomplished by trial and error. The more you work at this, and see results, the better you get at knowing when to do something and when to stay out of the way.

We will often try to do the Universe's part simply because we haven't learned how to trust. There were many times in the years after my accident, when I was reconnecting with my faith in God, that something would happen and I would cry out for God's help. After the help arrived, it was as if I had brushed myself off, told God I was okay, had things under control, and would take over from there. Only I wasn't in control, and it would only be a matter of time before I got squashed again (figuratively). So soon I would be crying out once more for help. Once I realized I wasn't in control, things continued to get smoother in my life. It all comes down to trusting—and trusting means getting still within you.

The desires of our heart appear when we stop trying to do it all ourselves and allow the Universe to do its part. Don't question how it will manifest. That is the Universe's problem. Your objective is to state your desire, believe it, be still, and know it is done. Not that it *will* be done, but that it *is* done.

Be still and know that you can create whatever you desire. Whether it's abundance, health, peace, or the perfect relationship, you can do it! Focus on what you want instead of focusing on what you don't have or what's missing. Stand up, make a choice, and make it happen. Go beyond believing in The Law of Attraction; *know it exists* and that it's at your disposal at all times. Be clear on your intentions. Remember, whatever your desire is, it already exists. Being absolutely clear in what you want brings it forth.

Be still and maintain an attitude of gratitude. The more gratitude you have, the more things will manifest for you. Be grateful for what you have right now. I'm grateful to be able to write what you're reading at this moment. People who are in gratitude typically vibrate at a higher energy level. And it's all about energy, isn't it? Vibrating at higher energy will create a chain reaction for you to manifest your desires.

Chapter 10

Taking Out the Trash
(Living in the Moment)

ONE OF THE MOST IMPORTANT LIFE LESSONS I learned from my accident was the ability to live in the moment. The problem is, it took me several years after my accident to realize that I had learned it. It may sound easy to do, but this does take some discipline. I had spent my entire adulthood up until July 11, 1989 focused on the future. Working hard to build up my business was the most important thing to me. That always meant working toward a day in the future when I would be able to "stop and smell the roses."

That fateful July day changed my perspective forever. I realized my life could be over in a flash. Having spent all of it working toward something that may never happen was foolish. I had the present moment, and I was promised nothing more. Few of us know when we are going to die. It could be next week, it could be next year, or it could be 50 years from now. We have all heard that we should live every day as if it were our last. In essence, if you do that, you will truly live your life.

Savoring the Moment

During my three months of hospitalization, I learned how to compartmentalize each day as a means of psychological survival. That means I focused on that day and that day alone.

Every moment you are consciously experiencing provides extraordinary joy and bliss.

It took all I had to survive that. Although it started out in a bad way, it actually was good. If I could put behind me what may have happened the day before or didn't think about what may or may not happen the next day, it was easier to function in the given day. I had a heightened experience of focusing on the now. I learned this technique, however, in the controlled environment of a hospital where I felt safe. Once discharged and back in the "real world," I began to fear the past because of what had happened. I also started to fear my uncertain future. The ultimate fear came from the realization that I wasn't in control. For a type "A" personality with huge personal walls built around him, this was hard to swallow. I had always been in control; at least I thought I was. The realization that I had no control, years after the accident, allowed me to think back on the day-to-day environment I had learned to appreciate while cooped up in the hospital.

Learning to "be in the now" provides incredible results. Every moment you are consciously experiencing provides extraordinary joy and bliss. I truly believe these uncontrolled moments of bliss are a connection with the Divine. Being in the moment allows Universal Intelligence the opportunity to provide you with insight. Being focused on the failures of the past or fears of the future doesn't allow this to happen.

Living in the now is being present with our senses in this precise moment in time. If we're focused on the past or the future, we can't enjoy the only thing we have, which is *right now.* So empty the trash in your head. Clear out the beatings you gave yourself over past transgressions. Clear out the fears you have about tomorrow.

One of the greatest quotes related to living in the present comes from Eckhart Tolle, author of *The Power of Now*: "Focus your attention on the Now and tell me what problems you have at this moment." What problems *do* you have at this particular moment in time? (I didn't think you had any either.)

Worry is *not* an action word. Maybe you did think of a problem you have in this very moment. Well, if you know you could do something specific about it and it would go away, *do it!* If you don't know what you can do to change it, *let it go!* If you know that if this happens and that happens you may have to do something specific in the future, let that go as well. You may never have to do anything about it. So why ruin your day over things that may never happen? Your worry will not change it, so release the concern and consider that in the moment you have no problems.

Now I know that this is easier said than done. But I also know from a personal perspective that the moment I realize I'm worrying about something in the future or mentally licking my wounds over some past transgression, it is my mind wandering. When I can bring myself to the present moment, I begin to realize that it's all mind chatter. Ask yourself whether this perceived problem is serving your higher good or is it just worry? As you begin to realize how safe you are right at this moment, and that it is okay with you, your preconceived notions will melt away. *Catch the thought. Look at it. Let it go.*

I've come to realize that my childhood had a tremendous effect on my ability to live in the present. I always coped by telling myself that when I got older, I wouldn't have to put up

Warren Zevon's Final Lesson

If you've been able to learn to be in the moment naturally, I commend you. Some of us need a little "attention-getter," so to speak, to allow us to see things differently. Some of us have to face our own mortality in order to see it. Warren Zevon is one of these individuals.

A Grammy-Award-winning singer/songwriter, Zevon was often known for his unique take on things, and this was certainly reflected in his songwriting. I always appreciated his dark sense of humor. In 2002, at the age of 55, Zevon was diagnosed with inoperable lung cancer and given six months to live. On October 30 of that year, Zevon was the only guest on the *Late Show with David Letterman*. He and Letterman had become friends over the years, and the musician had filled in as band leader many times when Paul Shaffer was out of town.

When asked how things had become since the diagnosis, Zevon related that one of the main lessons he had come to appreciate was to "put more value on every minute" and to "enjoy every sandwich." I think the sandwich comment is an incredible metaphor. If we could enjoy every sandwich of our lives, our days would be filled with joy and happiness. We would begin to live authentic lives, be who we are truly meant to be. On September 7, 2003, Zevon succumbed to the cancer.

In an interview with *Rolling Stone* magazine in September 2008, Letterman said one of the most difficult moments of his life was backstage with Zevon after that show. While backstage, Zevon packed up his guitar, used many times on *Late Night,* turned, and gave the instrument to Dave, asking him to take care of it. In that magazine article, Dave reflected on the fact that he broke down sobbing when the guitar was given to him. The thought of one human being facing mortality and carrying himself like Zevon did was a credit to who the man was and had become.

with anything from anyone. *I would be the one in charge.* The problem with that line of thinking is that the mind's always in the future causing needless anxiety and worry. And the ego loves that.

I was rarely able to enjoy anything happening in the moment because I was too consumed with worrying about the future. I see it so clearly now. In my early adulthood, it was the same way. There's nothing wrong with having future goals, but we need to live every moment to the fullest without worrying about what may or may not happen. Staying present while doing the best you can do in every moment will lead you to where you want to go.

Finding Focus

Many of us who meditate have the ability to block out the chatter and focus during the period when we're meditating. What about the rest of the time? It's in our waking moments when we need to focus on the specific task at hand, no matter how mundane. Next time you're doing something you love, notice how focused you are, how easily you block out everything. It's as if time doesn't exist. Some people call this "being in the flow." I love when I have the ability to experience moments like that.

Focusing on the task at hand allows us to live in the present moment. As boring as it may sound, training yourself to operate in this way will open unimaginable bliss in the simplest of experiences. There's no fear in the present because nothing can harm us in the here and now. An added bonus in focusing on the task at hand, rather than rushing through it to get on to something else, is that it helps us appreciate it more and do a better job. This is always better and more rewarding than doing it twice.

Unfortunately for many of us, staying in the moment is often an extremely difficult habit to sustain. Yet when you do learn how to focus on one thing at a time, you will begin to see yourself accomplishing more. You'll find yourself feeling less stress and tension than you used to feel worrying about a million other things that you had no need to worry about. The more this becomes a way of life, the more profoundly you'll see change within. You will eventually begin to see the focus of your desire becoming more intense and more readily attainable.

By focusing on the present moment, past hurts are not allowed to fester. You will realize that they are in the past, not real, and unable to hurt you. As a result, it will be easier for you to forgive and unburden yourself from the chains that hold you in check. But don't stuff hurts back down when they arise. Look them over, recognize that they're part of the past, forgive the other person, forgive yourself for hanging on to them, and let the hurts go.

Conversely, focusing on the present prevents fear, worry, and anxiety about the future from creeping in. I would like to share an example of this with you and why it is so important. Recently, I was asked to speak with a twenty-five-year-old man in a Connecticut hospital who broke his back in a construction accident. When I called this young man, we spoke for a while about what he could expect to happen. Obviously, I had been through a similar ordeal, and he was eager to know everything I could share with him. I totally understand and appreciate how scared he was. But every time I would explain something, I always brought him back to the present moment and encouraged him to focus on today and to do the best he could in the now. Neither of us knows what will happen to him tomorrow, but miracles occur in the present moment. And just for the time I was blessed to be able to connect with him and encourage him, he seemed calmer and more at ease. Was it because of what I said? I think it was because we focused on the now and the fear and anxiety of the future dissipated.

Releasing Blame & Worry

Remember the effect that ego has on us? It holds onto our perceived failures to gain a hold on us. By continuing to blame others for our perceived problems, we are giving away our power. You shouldn't blame others, nor should you blame yourself. When something happens that isn't what you intended, look the situation over and determine what you can do better the next time. Take a perceived failure and turn it into a learning experience.

> By continuing to blame others for our perceived problems, we are giving away our power.

Life is full of learning experiences. If you watch a toddler do something for the first time, they always fail. But they pick up the effort again and do it over, and then if they fail, they do it again. After they do it right, they still spend time doing the same thing, in the same way, while affirming to themselves that they now know how to do it. As adults, we may not have the need to continuously repeat the same situation again and again; however, we do need to learn from our failures so we have more knowledge the second time. Blame robs us of that opportunity.

If we truly live in the moment, we don't worry and have no need to feel anxious about anything. Once we learn to set forth our intentions to the Universe, we need to trust that what we are looking for already exists, and that it's becoming part of our reality. When we do that, there's no need to worry. Don't become attached to the outcome. I can't tell you how many times I used to say to myself, "I'll be happy when ..." I never was because it either didn't happen, or if it did, it didn't satisfy me. I would then wonder, "What's next?"

The most important thing you can do is be present and involved in whatever is happening at this moment. Sometimes our resistance to what's happening now prolongs the situation and makes it seem much worse than it actually is. I have occasionally found that I was resisting something, and when I thought about it, I couldn't find a reason why I was so dead set on having it my way. When I stopped being so resistant and let it go its own direction, I found that direction much more satisfying. Sometimes we have ideas that are stored in our subconscious, and they pop up to tell us that we have to think certain thoughts without consideration to their logic. As a result, we then can act in a way that may not be our best option.

> *Sometimes our resistance to what's happening now prolongs the situation and makes it seem much worse than it actually is.*

Targeting Potential

Potential can inevitably be our own worst enemy. For years, I felt I had incredible potential. If I kept focused on tomorrow, it would only be a matter of time before my potential would come to fruition. The day of the accident, my life as I knew it was over. How could that be? I had so much potential!

We all have the ability to do incredible things. Most times, our biggest successes come when we step outside of our comfort zone. To move out of our comfort zone provides us with the opportunity to take intelligent risks. We have a choice to either take those risks and move forward, or to stay in our comfort zone and experience regret. The good news is that being in the present will provide us with the answers we need to move ahead.

Potential can be dangerous. It can keep us stuck where we currently are. It's as if life continues to dangle the proverbial carrot in front of us. We maintain the notion of potential but never quite have the ability to take a bite. We are "comfortable" with our existing conditions no matter how painful or dissatisfying they are because we know that someday—not now, but someday—we will reach our potential.

The only way to live your potential is to live fully in the present moment. *Be yourself.* You are a perfect being as you are right now, so quit beating yourself up. There's no need to impress anyone. You have the power within to do incredible things. *Allow it to happen.*

There's a great Zen story that, when analyzed, reveals everything there is to know about living in the moment and seizing potential. One day while walking in the jungle, a man encounters a tiger. Fearing for his life, he begins to run as the tiger is in hot pursuit. The man comes to the edge of a cliff, and seeing that the tiger is about to jump on him, he notices a thick vine hanging over the edge of the cliff. Grabbing the vine and holding on with both hands, the man begins to climb down. Halfway toward the ground, the man looks up and sees the tiger angrily peering at him from the top of the cliff. Unfortunately, the man then looks down and sees another tiger staring up at him and growling, awaiting his arrival at the bottom. There's no place to go; he's stuck between the two!

The representation of the tiger at the top is the past. Should we decide to dwell on the past, we will continually beat ourselves up for not being able to do things as well as we (our ego) think we should. What we need to do is to learn to let go of these negative experiences. Yes, if there was a lesson to be learned, remember that, but let *the experience itself* go. It was just an experience anyway. If we hold onto the past, it allows the tiger at the top of the cliff to have opportunities to bite us. The tiger at the cliff's edge also represents the notion that we cannot go back in time. Quit thinking, "If I could only go back and change ___(whatever)___, my life would be so much better." Forgive yourself and forget it. For those who missed that—forgive yourself and forget it! Time is linear and moves in one direction—*forward.*

Now the tiger at the bottom of the cliff represents the future or the unknown. This includes all our hopes and dreams, as well as our potential setbacks. It is tomorrow, and we don't know what tomorrow may bring. If we continue to climb down our vine, we are just looking ahead and merely speculating about what may or may not happen when we really have no control over it anyway. These unrealistic fears do not allow us to relax and let Universal Intelligence enter (to provide the answers we seek). When we are unable to do that, we become full of tension and stress.

If you think it can't get any worse for our friend, think again. As the man looks up, he sees rats starting to gnaw on the vine. He keeps trying to shoo the rats away, but they return and resume their chewing. As the rats continue to gnaw, the vine becomes weaker and weaker. This represents the fact that time continues on and each moment brings us a little closer to death. At some point, when the vine breaks, the man will plummet to a certain end. In the same way, as our time on the vine draws near, we too will be facing the tiger. We may think we can shoo away the rats and slow death's approach, but time slows for no one. The ego's biggest fear is death, but none of us is immune from the tiger at the bottom of the cliff.

At about the lowest point in the entire experience, the man looks straight ahead in front of him and sees a plump, ripe strawberry within his reach. While holding on to the vine with one hand, he stretches out with the other hand and plucks the strawberry growing out of the cliff. With one tiger above, one tiger below, and rats gnawing on the vine, the man tastes the strawberry and finds it absolutely delicious. Despite all the apparent dangers surrounding him, he is able to seize the moment and savor it!

This strawberry represents the extraordinary beauty of *the now*, the present moment. It is available for all to experience, but who among us takes it in fully on a regular basis? Most of us just go through the motions waiting for a "strawberry" to appear. Well, they are all around you. Seize one and savor it. You will appreciate the miracle of existence. You will notice the beauty in *everything*.

Now we've noted that the man's position on the vine between the tigers represents the present. He is suspended in midair just as we are suspended between the past and the future. But even the present moment is an elusive concept. As soon as we point to a present moment and label it, it has already become the past!

One other interesting concept related to this story is the vine itself. The vine represents life in the material world. Just as the man holds onto the vine with both hands, we too stubbornly hang on to life. We think it is our survival. From the moment we enter into this life, we have no other choice but to begin living it. Why not live it fully from moment to moment!

Seeking Awareness

We can't pick up on metaphors, such as those in the story, unless we are aware of the symbols in our lives. Most people need to learn how to notice. We need to overcome our lack of awareness. Most of us live each day repeating the past or worrying about the future. Meanwhile, we don't realize that all we really have is *this* moment. Even if we do realize that we only have *the now*, many of us are afraid to truly enjoy it, and we need to learn how. We need to learn how to let go and reach out.

In the story, if the man had seen the strawberry but held onto the vine tightly with both hands, the enjoyment of the moment (tasting the strawberry) wouldn't have happened. How many times in our own lives do we wish to experience something differently, only to allow it to pass by because we're too afraid to let go of the vine with one hand and reach out. Notice the metaphor here; holding onto the vine tightly with both hands represents a need to have attachments with material items. With that attachment, you cannot let go and enjoy the present.

Even if we do realize that we only have the now, many of us are afraid to truly enjoy it, and we need to learn how.

A story in Luke 18:21-23 (NSRV) tells of a young rich man who asks Jesus what he needs to do to become a follower. Jesus responds by telling the man to give away all his possessions and follow him. The man couldn't do it, and he stayed on the side of the road weeping. I too had become attached to my possessions. They defined me. My possessions were who Bill Shaner was. Once that building collapsed, I was given the opportunity to learn who I was in a new and deeper way. One of the great lessons I learned after the accident was to reach out and enjoy each day.

Life grows and continues to grow. You need to get out of your norm and learn to take chances, to expand your horizons. Learning to live in the present can take a little work. However, once you learn it, this is easy and exciting.

Learn what your attachments are. Answering the following two questions will allow you to formulate the path you were destined to follow. First ask: "What can I let go of?" The expensive sports car you have to have to make you feel whole isn't going to do it. The big house needed to impress your friends isn't going to do it either. Letting go of attachments allows you to live life to the fullest. Then ask yourself: "What are my innermost interests?" Discover the things that already keep you in the present. If you can't think of any, ask God or the Universe for guidance in finding them.

The more you learn to live and experience the present moment, the sooner you will begin to realize how easy it can be to stop dwelling on the past or continuously worrying about the future. You will begin to experience peace.

Chapter 11

The Role of the Observer

It's all mind stuff. Everything in our reality is influenced by what we think about and how we think about it. How well we understand this and, more importantly, how we use it to our benefit determines how successful we are with our life experience. This is why it's so important to realize that we have a major influence in how our life turns out.

It's not by chance, or through a roll of the dice, unless you choose it to be that way. Learn to get into the role of the observer and you can take your life in directions you never thought possible. You have the choice to look at your circumstances or to look at the causes of your circumstances. By being aware, you have the opportunity to have a causal effect on your circumstances and to change them to your advantage.

In my own life, as I become more aware, I find that the Universe compels me to move forward with my experience. As I focus on this, people and circumstances appear and disappear, allowing me to make conscious choices. The key is to become conscious of the choices that we have at our disposal at all times.

Many different theories and studies exist on what has been called levels of awareness or levels of consciousness. I like to use the term "Levels of Awareness" with these four subcategories:

The 4 Levels of Awareness

- Unconsciously Unaware
- Consciously Unaware
- Consciously Aware
- Unconsciously Consciously Aware

The psychology profession has been studying the "levels of consciousness" since the beginning of the 20th century. Psychiatrist Sigmund Freud identified three different parts of the mind, based on our level of awareness. He called them the *conscious mind*, the *preconscious mind*, and the *subconscious mind*, which have been described earlier in the book.

The key is to become conscious of the choices that we have at our disposal at all times.

Prior to Freud, psychologist William James wrote about our physical, mental, and spiritual selves, as well as the ego. Within the past several decades, there has been a debate as to the various definitions of the term "consciousness" and its effect on humankind. It has only been a short period of time in the existence of human beings during which the study of why we do what we do has been undertaken.

Psychologist Abraham Maslow was one of the first in his field to theorize that humans are motivated by needs and that we all operate with some sort of hierarchy related to our needs. The lowest level in humans is the primal need of survival. Once we develop the ability to master survival, the next level is to feel secure. We achieve this by establishing relationships with others. Humans continue to rise through the levels as they meet each basic need. The next level is the need for self-esteem. Once a strong sense of self-esteem, or self-worth, is developed, the focus shifts to consciousness and on to self-actualization.

During this process, humans learn to release fears that prevent them from becoming independent. Self-actualization ultimately allows humans to be free. So the more we learn to become self-aware, the more we see the conscious choices available to us, rather than not being aware of the infinite possibilities that exist. If we don't grow in awareness, we become stuck in our current situation.

Self-actualization ultimately allows humans to be free.

Levels of Awareness

Human needs and the parts of the mind connect with the levels of awareness. How observant we are in the present moment is dependent on our level of awareness.

Unconsciously Unaware is best described as a state of being asleep. If we aren't conscious, we are, for the lack of a better term, asleep. No information is processed at this level. We simply exist. Unfortunately, I think there are people out there who live their entire lives in this state. We need to be awake in order to direct our attention outward or inward. In a state of sleep, this is not possible.

Consciously Unaware is a state in which we are not asleep. We are able to process information from the environment and respond as necessary. In this state, people appear to be awake and go to their jobs, interact with others, make dinner, and so on. They are in a conditioned state and react to situations with mechanical responses. These individuals can experience perceptions, thoughts, and sensations, but they are not "aware" that these are occurring, hence the mechanical response.

Most people live at this level. They interact with others, live their lives as they have been taught, but the key detail is that they don't monitor these actions. It's all merely about the experience of going through the motions and not realizing that there are reasons behind it. They may have a sense of constantly feeling unsettled. They might have a job that they don't enjoy; however, when they realize that life is calling them to truly live, they're too far in debt from a mortgage, car payments, and credit cards to believe they have a way out. Rather than work on this opportunity to create real life, they run and hide and continue with their meager existence.

Despite dissatisfaction with their lives, they find every excuse possible to avoid the action necessary to leave their familiar lives. "I cannot live on what I would make if I did what I enjoy. I'm too tired to do any more than I do. I don't have time for a hobby. I make just enough to cover bills. I wish I could get away, but money is too tight."

Consciously Aware is a level that allows us to relate to the environment and therefore we are able to look at the world and life differently. Life begins to take on amazing changes once we learn that we have the ability to be aware of "self." In this state, we pay attention to self as object. It's seeing the self as object without any justification or condemnation. We are simply being aware of self. Thus begins our journey as an observer. We learn to watch without judgment and make choices that benefit us while keeping emotion out of the equation.

Suppose you have a choice about ice cream. To be truly non-judgmental, you may choose chocolate. But you choose it at that moment without making a judgment about other flavors. Nor would you be making a choice about the next time you choose a flavor of ice cream. You wouldn't say to yourself, "I like it better than strawberry." You would just say, "Chocolate sounds good right now."

Being consciously aware allows you to watch your emotions, motives, and perceptions. You see things for what they are. Without old emotional hurts or judgments from the past, you rise above those issues and consciously make the decision best for you. Ultimately, being consciously aware allows you to control your destiny. And isn't that what the human experience should be about?

Unconsciously Consciously Aware is a state in which we have the ability to see everything freely without the need to identify with anything or to make any judgments. It is what it is—nothing more and nothing less. When we judge something, it's an indication that we have identified with it or not. The ego has become involved.

When you operate in this state, if even for only a few moments at a time, you will notice how many people are asleep at the wheel. By noticing this, you're not sitting in judgment, just making an observation. As you move toward this level, like with anything else, you will be a work-in-progress. I know this kind of growth has helped me make some profound changes in how I see the world and operate within it. Fear has been replaced, for the most part, with an inner calmness that I had only imagined could be possible.

In the consciously aware state, you might say, through your awareness, "I feel angry." You're not just saying it as a response to a stimulus, but rather an inner knowing—almost as if observing the behavior in another. You were aware and didn't judge it or condemn it. In your awareness of being aware state, you might say, "I am aware of the fact that I am angry."

Certainly anger can be judgmental and condemning, but we're not talking about that. We're talking about when we are aware of having the feeling and being able to get outside of it, to observe it as if someone else were telling you a story about something that angered them. You're not doing this to get charged and take sides; you're just observing. You may want to look at it from all sides and think about how you might see this situation in a different way.

The Role of Observer in a Crisis

When I moved back to the west coast of Florida three years ago, I did it for business reasons and got involved in a business startup opportunity. This deal went horribly wrong in less than one year. I lost a substantial amount of money and had incurred a sizeable amount of debt. Once I stopped allowing my ego to beat me up and tell me how worthless and stupid I was, I began to re-focus on being the observer of this situation. I looked at it for what it was without judgment. As I continued to work at it and continued to see it for what it was, I was able to clearly see many choices that I had. I was able to take a path that required hard work and self-sacrifice (my choice). Within two years, I had the entire mess (statement not judgment) cleaned up.

When you're able to observe like this, you can easily think about why your emotion is as such and change the thought process that put you in that state. Being unaware of the fact that you're angry can make for quite a miserable day for you, as well as others around you.

While being in the role of the observer, we have the opportunity to truly change our experience of life. Focus on the ability to observe situations and the emotions connected to them. Don't judge or identify with the situation. When we judge and identify, it usually brings along some preconceived notion of pain. By observing things as they are, we can move through life without the burden of the unnecessary baggage

we all create and carry around. Being the observer allows us to make choices free from all
that baggage. It allows us to operate in this
experience with a clear mind and create what
we want.

Focus on the ability to observe situations and the emotions connected to them. Don't judge or identify with the situation.

We can get a substantial edge on life when
we learn the lesson of living in the moment
(covered in the previous chapter) along with developing the
ability to observe situations from the outside. Observing provides the opportunity to change our circumstances and create
experiences we choose rather than having life or someone
else decide for us. I'd like to suggest a movie that demonstrates what I'm talking about, and it's actually fun to watch.

Learning from a Movie

The movie focuses on how repetition of the same challenges
can aid growth. Have you ever noticed how we sometimes repeat the same patterns over and over in our lives? The same
mistakes in the partners we choose in our relationships, the
same wrong career choices. Plenty of us repeat these issues until we figure out what we're doing wrong. The ones who figure
out the errors are the ones who have a better chance at success.
Hints are all over the place for us to see.

This is exactly what Bill Murray faces in the 1993 comedy
Groundhog Day. Murray plays Phil, an arrogant weather fore-
caster sent to Punxsutawney, Pennsylvania, to do a broadcast on
the local groundhog and whether it will see its shadow. A bliz-
zard forces Phil to remain in town, and he wakes up the next
morning only to realize it's the same day all over again. Everything that occurred the previous day happens again. Phil winds
up stuck in town with the same events occurring day after day
after day after day. Ever been there before? *I know I have!*

Many times, we are in situations that repeat themselves, and at first, we may seem bewildered at how things are turn-ing out. Then eventually, we may begin to play games with our circumstances rather than work at resolving the core issues. This only prolongs the agony. Until we uncover the rea-sons that we continue to create the same cir-cumstances in our own life, we will face the same results—often wondering why. Once we do see what's in a given situation and realize we have the power to change our thoughts, which will change our results, we'll begin to see our world change.

Until we uncover the reasons that we continue to create the same circum-stances in our own life, we will face the same results—often wondering why.

Phil finally takes control of the day rather than letting the circumstances of the day take control of him. We should learn to do that, too. Our lives will change just as his did, and this type of experience will disappear.

Once Phil accepts his situation, he realizes the power in this and in not trying to force things. By pointing this out, I'm not implying that we should acquiesce to everything that happens in our lives. On the contrary, we should work at moving things forward as much as possible to our advantage. The fine line in creativity is knowing when to accept things as they are and work with the opportunity presented in what-ever situation that may arise.

I have seen this movie many times and watch it every chance I get. If you have never seen the film, I suggest you watch it. In fact, I suggest you watch *Groundhog Day* over and over. Every time I watch it, I come away with the reminder that there are times in everyone's lives when we are in this type of nonproductive repetitive cycle. We stay there until we learn whatever lesson we're supposed to learn. It seems that once we learn the lesson, we're allowed to move forward.

Some of us have a negative cycle that lasts *for years*. For others, it can last forever! This movie shows us that if we can learn to accept life and the situation we're in (it doesn't mean it has to be forever), life can cease to be a problem. It allows us to become real with ourselves and compassionate with others. Until we change our circumstances, the results will remain the same. Once we change our perspective, our circumstances will begin to change at that very moment. Our outer world is a reflection of our inner world. Once you understand this principle, your life will begin to flow.

Chapter 12

Science vs. Religion

AS HUMAN BEINGS, WE HAVE ALWAYS BEEN inquisitive about our surroundings, since the beginning of time. We're always trying to figure out why things are the way they are. So why, then, has there been this chasm between science and religion? I know, in my own circumstances, whenever I may have questioned the existence of God, it never had anything to do with science. Being extremely left brained and analytical and needing everything to make logical sense still does not deter me in my belief of a Higher Power in the Universe. To me, it makes perfect sense that science and religion can, and should, coexist; in fact, they could be one and the same. The Universal power that created life provides science the opportunity to define, quantify, and explain it.

Let's look at both camps.

Matters of Faith

To some, the Bible is the word of God—period. End of story. They believe that the Bible is without error because God inspired its authors. I have even heard it described by one preacher as "God-breathed," meaning every word of the Bible was actually spoken by God. If it's not in the Bible, it must be secular and not of God. If it's not in the Bible, it must be an anti-God thing.

Others believe that the Bible contains the word of God but that it's not free of errors. For example, God is love and yet an angry God, so why is anger a sin for us and perfection in God? This is a contradictory example of how some perceive confusion, or errors, in the Bible.

The Universal power that created life provides science the opportunity to define, quantify, and explain it.

And still others believe that the Bible contains much that is spiritually positive, and that is how they interpret it. In this theology, there's no need to think you have to hide from God. I fall into the third category.

Religion is concerned with matters of faith. The crux is that God created all and exists in all. This has been handed down orally generation to generation, recorded by scribes into the Bible, or revealed to us through prayer.

Analyzing the Evidence

Science deals with the study of nature and how it works. Science is based on an analysis of evidence. Typically, first there is a hypothesis. That is a guess, but generally an educated guess. Studies are performed which prove, or disprove, a given theory. Science stays away from matters of morality, spirituality, or the existence of God.

Science is black and white. It is either proven or it's questionable. A lack of evidence doesn't mean it doesn't happen; it only means it's not proven. Therefore, it has no cause that would ensure it would happen again in precisely the same way. Once something has happened, it's highly probable that science can explain what happened and possibly why. Science can also determine whether there's enough evidence to conclude if it was random or if it will happen again when duplicating the same circumstances. Ultimately, from the scientific point of view, we encounter a problem when someone thinks his own religion is the only true belief and everything else (other faiths and science) have flawed belief systems. There is then a contention and a loss in the one true foundation of all religions: *God is love.* Love is all God has ever claimed to be!

As far back as ancient Greece, people debated many of the same philosophical questions we still discuss today, such as "Why are we here?" The Greeks also studied the Universe. They watched celestial movements, which brought about the development of astrology. Our development and study of mathematics and physics today are a direct result of astronomy and astrology.

Fast forward to the 16th century and you see an entirely different story. In Europe, the church was the end all and be all—the sole power over people. The word of the church was law. When Copernicus suggested in 1543 that the sun, rather than the Earth, was the center of the Universe, the church was outraged. How dare someone contradict a belief of the church? It forbade the people from even considering this theory. Galileo refined this concept in the early 1600s. And for his effort, the church put him on trial for heresy and ultimately placed him under house arrest until his death.

Many other scientific advancements occurred subsequent to Galileo's. Sir Isaac Newton is one example. Newton's breakthroughs in physics stood for centuries as the only correct theory to be followed. As science continued its expansion and began diverging from the church, a rift developed between the two. And after Darwin, the rift became a chasm.

Scientists from Galileo on described the Universe as a non-living world of inanimate objects. The turn of the 20th century began to shake things up again. People such as Albert Einstein and Neil Bohr, to name but a couple, began the study of matter and started to unlock a further mystery. The development of quantum theory suggests that this is not a material world; instead, as we look at smaller and smaller particles, we see that they dissipate into pure energy. What does all this mean? It shows that the physical world is non-physical. That is quite a shift in perspective!

Thousands and thousands of years ago, science and religion co-existed beautifully. Early scientists believed that God had given them a world to be appreciated and studied, perhaps in a way similar to how theologians studied God through scripture. Then we begin to see the pendulum swing. The church for many centuries tried to control science. Perhaps it was afraid of what might be found. Ultimately, as the pendulum began to swing back to the side of scientific study, scientists thought their study of hypotheses based on reason and methodology was sufficient. Therefore, they had no need for God. Then the discovery of quantum theory began to swing the pendulum back. Things were not as they seemed. They never are!

If you understand the concept of quantum theory, you see at its core a cloud of possibilities—depending on how you view it at any given moment. If you believe that to be your truth, then any situation you may currently be in has many possible outcomes. And those outcomes are determined by the choices you make. Whichever possibility you choose will determine your view of reality.

Life is not left to chance. If life were a random series of events that are all out of our control, God would not be necessary. Similarly, our experiences go deeper and beyond the limits of science. Explanations of processes of how life operates and interrelationships therein described by physics, chemistry, and biology all have their limitations. Experiences of love, of beauty, of truth take us beyond what science can explain. We have the choice of how we interact with things and other people. We have the opportunity to have a say in how our experiences will turn out. God intertwines with the world of science, and both are at our disposal.

Life is not left to chance. If life were a random series of events that are all out of our control, God would not be necessary.

God works through the various laws of nature, and we can tap into His magnificence in order to create the reality of our dreams. We have discussed the Law of Attraction, for example, in great detail and what can be achieved by practicing it. And who among us hasn't experienced the Law of Cause and Effect (Karma)? We also have the free will to choose to allow these natural laws to dictate our existence. The parting of the Red Sea has been explained by science in many different ways. There is evidence that it happened with chariots strewn along a path under the water. How can that be? How can it be a miracle and a predictable phenomenon at the same time? The phenomenon is scientific to be sure. Had it not happened at the exact moment when it did, we would call it a phenomenon and think, "Hmm, isn't that interesting …" and leave it at that. Because it can be scientifically explained and it happened at the precise moment when it was needed doesn't negate the notion of it being a miracle from God and a natural phenomenon that can be explained by science at the same time.

I believe God sustains creation in its automatic form. He also allows us the opportunity to have a say in how we wish to create things. If you had told me 20 years ago that this would be my belief, I would have told you that you were absolutely out of your mind.

Some followers of strong religious beliefs will feel threatened by science: the same science that has provided them with many of the material comforts they currently enjoy. As long as they can call science secular, they feel safe; those are the things that are explained and yet hold no significance for good or evil. Science provides an accurate description of our physical environment. It is not an absolute system of belief. By combining our ancient spiritual traditions with the best that modern science has uncovered, we have the ability to have a unified view of the world rather than the dualistic concept people have had for centuries. Science gives us the opportunity to study and describe natural laws set in motion by a Universal energy. God uses the processes of our physical world to act upon our behalf. This is where science and religion, although using different approaches, both propose to explain what we see and what we cannot see. Too often we cannot see with our imperfect human vision God's handprint upon our lives. But rest assured, He is there.

By combining our ancient spiritual traditions with the best that modern science has uncovered, we have the ability to have a unified view of the world rather than the dualistic concept people have had for centuries.

PART III
WHAT I NOW KNOW

"We haven't begun to understand the power
that God has created within the
human being and within life."

~ Dr. Robert H. Schuller

Chapter 13

Why Not Create Your Reality?

THERE ARE TWO IMPORTANT THEOREMS TO know and understand, although they may not be in sync with what you were taught as a child. First, everything in our Universe is energy. *Everything.* Everything you see, feel, and touch is energy. This book you are holding is pure energy. Science has proven this through quantum physics, which you can learn more about in any number of books dedicated to the subject. Scientists have discovered, and continue to discover, that no matter how small a particle they analyze (even subatomic), it is all a form of energy. What you see, feel, or touch is a solidified form or lower level of vibration occurring in the Universe. In the spiritual realm, negative energy is considered to be dense and heavy, therefore creating a lower level of vibration. If you have ever been introduced to a negative person and wondered why you felt some sort of bad energy, you know what I am talking about. Conversely, you enjoy hanging around positive people because you get a good feeling being in their presence. Their energy is lighter and vibrates at a higher level.

If you broke down everything you see into ever smaller particles, you would find that nothing is solid; rather, it is all energy. Furthermore, physicists, using particle accelerators (to take subatomic particles and smash them together), have discovered that results appear to exist only when someone is thinking about them. In other words, at the smallest of the small, an infinite number of possible results exists. What this means is that results occur for scientists based on their thought process, i.e., what result they may be thinking about.

If they can create the results they want in controlled experiments, what stops us from doing it with our lives? The answer is *nothing*. What you focus on, you create—whether it's good or bad. Therefore, creation of anything in the physical universe is determined by what kind of attention you place on it.

The second theorem is that there is one source of the energy that makes up all things. Some call this "God," some call it "the Universe." Whatever you wish to call it, we are all one with this Source, and it manifests itself in every living being. What does this mean and why should you care? Well, we create our reality with this energy.

Every thought you have is energy. Every thought generates like energy to bring those ideas into reality. Your thoughts, in conjunction with the Universal Laws discussed earlier, especially the Law of Attraction, determine your reality. Since everything is energy and vibrates accordingly, we can fix our thoughts on our desires and manifest them in the physical world. It is not happenstance.

A Matter of Focused Attention

As I look back on my journey, I see many instances that demonstrate how this works. I have also been able to see how it didn't quite work when I was unsure of what I really wanted. I have come to know this process as truth, and ultimately seeking truth is finding the meaning of life.

The key is to continually focus on what you want and not waver. As an analogy, put the book down for a moment and focus on something in front of you: a vase, a lamp, whatever. No matter who steps in front of you or tries to get your attention, never take your focus off of that object. This scenario represents the focus you need to manifest your desires.

Thought is the only power that can produce tangible results from the Universe.

Perhaps you've experienced thoughts manifesting into action. Have you ever thought about another person a lot, really focused your attention on them, and then suddenly you receive a call from them or they show up out of the blue? It happens to me a lot. In fact, there are times when I want to speak to someone, and rather than call them, I'll focus my attention on them and wait for the phone to ring. It works! Thought is the only power that can produce tangible results from the Universe. What you intend to create already exists; you just need to bring it into form.

Whatever you focus your attention on, you will attract, but it must be done properly. This is the Law of Attraction, and it represents the line separating successful people from daydreamers and wishful thinkers. This process has been around since the inception of time. Throughout the centuries, famous and successful people have used this process to better themselves and humankind as well.

Biblical References

Even the Bible provides instruction on focused attention. For instance, there's the well-known passage: "Ask, and it will be given to you; search, and you will find; knock, and it shall be opened for you. For everyone who asks receives, and everyone who searches finds, and for everyone who knocks, the door will be opened." (Matthew 7:7-8) My evolvement in spirituality has taught me that I am not separate from God (the Universe), but rather I am part of one energy on this planet. We are here to fully express our true godly selves, and that means to be successful and prosperous; to find peace and joy; to have meaningful interpersonal relationships; to enjoy perfect health.

Having said all that, I truly believe many of Jesus' quotes in the Bible actually reference the power of thought. "[Jesus] said to them, ' ...For truly I tell you, if you have the faith the size of a mustard seed, you will say to the mountain, move from here to there; and it will move; and nothing will be impossible for you.'" (Matthew 17:20) Notice it says that faith the size of a mustard seed will move a mountain. Imagine what you can do when you realize the total power within you!

Matthew 6:31-33 states, "Therefore, do not worry, saying 'What will we eat?' or 'What will we drink?' or 'What will we wear?' ... but strive first for the kingdom of God and his righteousness, and all these things will be given to you as well." Here Jesus notes that the kingdom of God is within you. Seek first this power that is in each and every one of us and learn to use it. Learn to contact it and draw it forth; your desires will be at your disposal.

"Whatever you ask for in prayer with faith, you will receive." (Matthew 21:22) Note the key word here is *faith*. This is your unyielding belief when your thought goes out into the Universe. We ask for many things, but for whatever reason, we feel we are not deserving of our desires and that manifestation is not a real option. The Universe will pick up on this. It wants to give you everything your thoughts focus on, and give it to you right now.

John 10:30 states, "The Father and I are one." God is not separate from us but one with us. That's pretty good odds that you'll be able to create your dreams—provided you believe in you. "Your faith has made you well; go in peace and be healed." (Mark 5:34) This is very personal for me, as I experienced it firsthand and will never forget it. With a 99 percent chance, according to doctors, that I would be paralyzed for the rest of my life, I connected with the life force of the Universe and showed everyone what one person can accomplish. Now I'm not saying that there wasn't a moment or two along the way where fear didn't begin to rear its ugly head, but my faith remained constant. My faith remained strong, and that pure connection allowed me the opportunity to walk again.

"So I tell you, whatever you ask for in prayer, believe that you have received it, and it will be yours." (Mark 11:24) *Ask. Believe. Receive.* Notice it doesn't say beg. You don't need to continually ask because you may not believe you deserve it. Just ask, truly believe, and it will manifest. Here Jesus is speaking about using the mind, which is the connection to the Universe that allows us to create our desires.

Spirituality has always professed that we create our reality. Science is continuing to draw that conclusion. Even religion seems to be headed in the direction of spirituality more so than the dogma that separates the church from a secular world. We create our reality through our conscious use of our thoughts. Whatever we focus our thoughts on has the ability to create people, events, and circumstances in our life.

Creating what we want is all about how we use our thought process. Life is not outside of your control. You have the power to determine your outcome—good or bad. So why not focus your thoughts on what you want and go after them?

The Basics

We all come from and will always belong to one Universal energy force. All physical life functions in accordance with natural laws. These two statements sum up all you need to

Quotes on the Power of Thought

- *"For as a man thinketh in his heart, so is he."* Proverbs 23:7

- *"All that we are is a result of what we have thought."* Buddha (563 BC–483 BC)

- *"Man is what he believes."* Anton Chekhov (1860–1904)

- *"The thing always happens that you really believe in; and the belief in a thing makes it happen."* Frank Lloyd Wright (1867–1959)

- *"Imagination is everything. It is the preview of life's coming attractions."* Albert Einstein (1879–1955)

- *"Whatever the mind of man can conceive, it can achieve."* Napoleon Hill (1883-1970)

Whether you know it or not, whether you believe it or not, your "life" at this moment has been created because of your thoughts. You have the opportunity to develop patterns that will assist you in getting what you want. Either that or you can continue to leave it up to chance. How great would it be if you knew this process to be absolute truth? You would lose all fear and doubt and begin to create exactly what you want out of life.

know. The rest is how we use it. If we believe that one Universal energy force exists, and that everything we see, feel, and touch is energy, then everything that exists came from that unified source. If we believe our thoughts are energy and are in alignment with this unified source, then the thing imagined by thought is produced in the real world. Therefore, if we can form an idea in our thoughts and hold fast to the idea as it goes out into the Universe, we can cause the idea to manifest in our physical world.

Everything invented by human beings, everything manufactured by us, everything ever designed by people all started out as an idea, a thought. The chair you are sitting on right now reading this book (or the bed you are lying on) was once a thought in someone's mind. What we think about, we ultimately bring about. What we focus on becomes our reality. Humankind has known this for years, as the quotations on the previous page attest.

Cleaning Out the Cobwebs

In order to create the life of our dreams, we need to do some mental house cleaning. First, stop listening to the naysayers. These people will tell you that this will not work, that it cannot be done. Rather than break well-engrained habits to set a new course, they would rather have everyone else around them be as miserable as they are.

Once you tune in to the concept of creating your reality, you'll be able to feel this negative energy in others. I can tell immediately upon meeting someone if they're a negative person. It oozes out of them, and I run as quickly as possible in the other direction! You may have friends like this who you have argued with or acquiesced to over the years. You may think you can change them or that you're the better person by being their friend and overlooking this one tiny flaw. I believe it's actually better to spend your time with like-minded people who are positive. You'll be amazed how much better your own life works when you spend more time with positive, happy, and peaceful people. Think of Christopher Columbus. He didn't listen to the naysayers around him. Instead, Columbus took along the people who believed in him and his goals, and he set out to change the world. The naysayers thought he would die and all those with him would be lost.

Transforming Limiting Beliefs

You must be honest with yourself when clearing out limiting beliefs. Ponder the following questions:

What are my current beliefs?
Which ones do not serve me?
Which ones do I know not to be true today?

The unhelpful beliefs need to be replaced with beliefs that you know to be true. These beliefs should be formulated in the affirmative with statements like "I have," "I enjoy," "I am" rather than statements like "I am not," "I hate," "I never get." If it helps, write the new beliefs out. Re-craft your statements in the affirmative and believe them because that's really who you are.

The proper mental work can make you wealthy, but more than that, it will enrich your life beyond measure: improve health, wealth, relationships, anything you can imagine. Much of the information out there today centers on instant gratification and getting rich. There's so much more than that. This process will help change the inner you for the better. What should come from this journey is that you make the most of yourself, for yourself, and for others. By doing that, you'll be helping to make this a better place for all. This process is the blueprint for your life. Understand it and go make a masterpiece.

I've had to spend a lot of time soul-searching the reason I believe the things I do. I have also spent a lot of time working to eliminate self-defeating beliefs. Beliefs are just thoughts. And similar to how our thoughts have the power to create, our belief system is why we are currently experiencing the now.

Many of my childhood thoughts became my beliefs, setting me up for merely getting by through a lot of my adulthood. Whenever I would get into debt, my thoughts were not of abundance but rather trying to get back to even. I always focused on the future, not the now. When you think about something as happening in the future, you never bring it to the now; it sits there like the donkey and the carrot. Boy was my thinking screwed up. The Universe will work just as hard to see you not have something (because you don't believe you deserve it) as it will in providing you what your wish is, knowing that you deserve it.

The Universe will work just as hard to see you not have something (because you don't believe you deserve it) as it will in providing you what your wish is, knowing that you deserve it.

The process of replacing a self-limiting belief is really very simple. However, it must be practiced until the new belief is engrained in your current belief system. If it is not, whatever you wish to attain will be limited to your inner belief system.

What Do You Really Want?

This is the $64,000 question. What is it you truly want? For most people, it's to become wealthy. Others wish to have vibrant health. Still others want love and romance. Whatever it is, finding a job, starting a business, buying a car or dream home, it is all possible when done properly. If you ask most people what they really, truly want, they will not be able to tell you. That is why they don't have it in their reality. Their request to the Universe is too fuzzy. Successful people unequivocally believe that they will succeed. They will not entertain the thought of failure. They will not even talk about the possibility of failure and what that might bring. It's not a consideration. What is the belief system you have about yourself?

The desire for more is the capacity for the Universe to seek fulfillment. Life seeks fuller expression. In order to achieve this, we must be explicitly clear about what it is we want. One simple caveat fits: Our purpose or desire should be in harmony with our core. You will know when you are in alignment.

Remember, the Universe simply responds with what you think about. If you think about lack, that is what the Universe hears and sends back to you. Whatever you believe in your core (with feeling) becomes your reality. You can sit there and think everything is great, but if you hold a sense of lack as your core belief then you are only kidding yourself. You must believe *deep in your core* that everything is great and then think about how great it is.

Questions for Clarifying Your Desires

What do I want to have?
What do I want to do?
What do I want to be?
Where do I want to go?
What is it I truly want from life?

Obviously, you want something because you don't have it—yet. You may want a meaningful relationship. Rather than focusing on filling the void in your life, focus on the wonderful qualities you have to offer a partner. Focus on what you can give to a partner who is looking for those exact qualities you have and who has the qualities you want in a partner. One of the fastest ways to find a partner is to be the person you are looking for; have the qualities you want in your partner and offer them.

I've learned to ask myself questions to define and refine what I really want. My approach started out in a linear fashion; however, as I became more confident with the process, I learned how to multitask with my requests. When I first began to realize the power I had within me, I would work on creating one thing at a time, such as a fabulous vacation. Once I saw what I could do, I began to work on many things at the same time. Not only the fabulous vacation, but building up my business, creating abundance and harmony in my life. All of them at the same time. When you begin to be able to do that, your world changes dramatically.

The Universe is willing to give to all equally and liberally. You need to specifically define your desires. So ask yourself the questions listed in the box on the previous page.

Think about these questions and contemplate your answers. It may take a little while because you may not really know what you want.

Let's say you want a new car. Ask yourself why you want it and how it will make you feel. What's the essence of wanting a new car? Do you want reliable transportation? Do you want it as a status symbol? Where will it take you? How will the car improve your life? Do you really want a new car, or is there anything else that would better suit your needs? As you contemplate your desires, it may be helpful to write down as much information about each area of your new life that you wish to have. It is sometimes amazing to look at something on paper and actually think it is something you really want. You may not emotionally feel you deserve it, and that is why you don't have it. There's no reason why you don't have it; you simply want it now and ask for it now. The past is the past. Now is now. Putting it on paper helps you realize it's something that you do deserve. As you write down what you desire, include all the details you can imagine about what you want. Remember, the key is, the more specific you are about something, the quicker the manifestation occurs.

The Universe is willing to give to all equally and liberally. You need to specifically define your desires.

As we begin to get quiet and listen to our inner voice, the things we desire will begin to enter. We can accomplish virtually anything, but we should remember that the desires that are in alignment with our God-given talents will be the most successful. Let me give you a personal example. I am extremely left-brained. I am analytical with everything. My brain works on the mathematical side of things. Although I can appreciate the artistic side of life, I have virtually no artistic abilities. That being said, I have always wanted to play the guitar and be in a band. I have taken lessons and taught myself the mechanics. I know the basics and the theory behind it, yet I cannot for the life of me play like Eddie Van Halen. As much as I believe you can create whatever you want, the more your desires are in alignment with your inner core (God), the greater the success you will enjoy.

Spend as much quality time as you can with yourself. Ask for inner guidance.

Spend as much time detailing your thoughts as possible. Get quiet and think, meditate, or whatever works for you. Spend as much quality time as you can with yourself. Ask for inner guidance. Go within and to the Source. There is an amazing plan for your life, and God wants to express Himself through you. You are a unique individual. There is no one who has ever come before or will come after who is you. It is time to create your niche.

More on Meditation

Meditation is critical in this process. These moments in the silence provide the answers or direction we seek. I found it was hard to entertain the thought of sitting and quieting my "normal mind." My mind races so fast that I thought it would be impossible to get to the silence. But I found that it's not impossible. Some people grasp it quickly. For others, it can be arduous. You may want to read about how to meditate. You may want to find a teacher. Find a way that works *for you.*

If you're questioning why you should learn to meditate, let me explain the many benefits it provides. Neuroscientists have found that people who meditate shift brain waves to different areas of the cortex—for example, from the right frontal stress-prone cortex to the calmer left cortex. This shift reduces the negative effects of stress, anxiety, and even mild depression. These same scientists also found less activity in the amygdale, where the brain processes fear. Research indicates that meditating brings about dramatic results in as little as a 10-minute session. Meditation has also been shown to help reverse heart disease, and it can reduce pain and enhance your body's immune system, making it more able to fight disease.

As much as we want to quiet the incessant mind chatter, we soon find that meditation may be difficult to master. Many times, I find it difficult to overcome this internal chatter, but you cannot give up. You must work at it until it feels right. Whether it works well for you the first time or not, you will benefit from the very first time. Just keep working at meditation and it will get better each time you do it.

Meditation strips us down to bare attention. *Whatever is is whatever is.* There's no judgment involved. With practice, it will bring about a higher level of self-acceptance and provide insight above oneself. It allows us to put aside attachment with the ego. We learn that during meditation we don't need to fix things, and we learn to accept things the way they are. Meditation also fosters a greater understanding of interconnectedness with others.

I know that many times the ego-driven part of my mind will try to attach itself to a problem I'm having. It follows that subconsciously I keep inviting those thoughts in. Until I stop the invitations, the thoughts will keep coming. So I work at making a conscious decision to stop these repetitive thoughts. Next, I try to look at thoughts as separate from myself. I know it is difficult to do because they seem to be such a strong part of our minds. If we look at thoughts as coming from the outside, they decrease in importance. If I continue having a problem eliminating thoughts, I use a technique of trying to discover the origin of the thought. By questioning the source, I develop the ability to accept or reject the thought. Then I'm not the victim any longer. The better I become with these steps, the faster I'm able to see a negative thought enter. Then when I refuse to follow it, I see it fade. That allows me the opportunity in the stillness to receive intuitive answers. The difference is a deep inner feeling, a knowing of what you need to do.

You'll master meditation much more easily by becoming a creature of habit. Try to use the same room, the same chair, and so forth. Once you have mastered the physical part,

A Preliminary Practice

The results of meditation can be phenomenal. Getting silent can be tricky, however. I know my efforts vary. It's really a lifelong practice. I was taught a little process at the beginning, and it did help me.

First, find a place where you can be alone and undisturbed. Sit straight up, but get comfortable. Allow your thoughts to roam as they normally do. Next, concentrate on sitting as absolutely still as possible for at least 15 minutes. Go longer if you can, especially after practicing this process a couple times. Continue practicing until it becomes second-nature. Take a week or two until you have it down because this becomes an important base to work from. It is essential to be able to control the body before you move forward.

the next step is to work on thought. Get into your position, but in addition to the physical control, work on inhibiting all thought. This will allow you to control all thoughts about fear and worry, and you'll begin to allow yourself to focus on thoughts only of your desires. You may be able to do this a few moments at a time, but the lesson here is to notice the extraordinary number of thoughts that try to enter your mind. Learning how to control these thoughts allows you to focus on what it is you want.

The ultimate meditation experience is to eliminate every thought. If a thought enters your mind, don't fight it, but allow it to dissipate. It's in the moments of true silence that answers come. The answers come from your core—not from the chatter in your head. You are directed on what to do, how to do it, and when it is to be done. Meditation is a connection with God.

Dreams, Visions & Choices

Make your dreams about what you want to create as big as possible. To the Universe, there's no difference in size. The Universe is abundant and unlimited. There are no shortages. Ask for what you want, as long as you believe it is possible for you to have it. When your purpose, or desire, harmonizes with the Universe, consider this a done deal.

The Universe provides abundance equally to all who ask. Therefore, operate from the plane of creating what you want rather than competing with others.

The Universe provides abundance equally to all who ask. Therefore, operate from the plane of creating what you want rather than competing with others. There's no need to take anything away from anyone. There's no need to cheat or take advantage of others to get what you want. You are a creator, not a competitor. Desires acquired through competition usually are not permanent and ultimately do not satisfy.

Once you learn to rise above the competitive plane and into the creative plane, things show up easily and you'll have a feeling of inner peace. Create your vision not from what appears to be a visible supply, but rather the limitless supply that's available from the Universe. Focus and express the desire of God within. You need to stop thinking that you don't deserve things or that you must sacrifice. I spent many years doing that, and it got me nowhere.

After describing your desires in as much detail as possible, don't worry about how they will come to pass. That's the Universe's job. That is what creation is all about. Most times when I focus on something I want, I have no idea how it will come about—including writing this book! It's amazing how miracles show up in unexpected ways when you put your request out.

Whether or not we realize it, we are constantly making choices. Our choices then define the direction of our lives. Many of these choices are made subconsciously, meaning we aren't even aware that we are making them. Every choice we make, no matter how small or large, has an effect on many other things in our life. The lesson to realize here is the importance of our conscious decision-making. It ultimately determines the level of success in creating the life you want.

We must also understand that every choice we make provides us the opportunity to make additional choices as we proceed along a certain path. It's how we make those additional choices that will determine the refinement of our ultimate reality. Try this to fully grasp this point: Visualize for a moment a quiet, still pond. Throw a stone into the water and watch the ripples radiate out from the center. The stone represents our original thought, and each ripple represents the further potential of whatever decision we make. Being the observer allows us to watch things unfold and decide in which direction to head with our future thoughts. It's clarity of mind that allows clarity of choice.

Our choices also have an effect on other choices. They have the potential to change other decisions, whether it's something as minute as where to buy your morning coffee or something as significant as purchasing a home. Let's take a look at the house analogy for a moment. Suppose your focus/

desire is on whether to pursue purchasing a newly built home. Once that choice has been made, your next choice will be where you wish to live. After that decision is made, you will need to decide who will build it and so forth. Your choices will determine the future of other choices. Our choices have far-reaching shifts in the movement of things for us, as well as for other people. Once the stone has been thrown into the pond, watch the ripples begin. Conscious decision-making allows us to systematically create the life we truly desire.

Positive Thinking vs. Having a Clear Vision

Now it's the Universe's turn, but you must still be a major player to get proper results. You need to continue to have a clear vision of what you desire, not just a positive attitude. It's nice to be positive, but that will not be enough. The problem with most people (including me from time to time) is that they're not clear about what they want. Putting out a concise request and holding a clear vision will help draw the Universal energy needed to bring the request about.

It's nice to be positive, but that will not be enough.

Having a clear vision will come in handy when the naysayers start to appear, and they will. When you break out of your norm and start to experience incredible results, people will become jealous. Also, most people don't like to change. They think it takes too much work or it's too hard. They would prefer to sit around and be a victim rather than change and become a victor. Most people would rather live in their own fear; it seems more comfortable. However, there's no limit to what you can accomplish, so don't sell yourself short. If I listened to the doctors after my accident, I firmly believe I would still be in a wheelchair today.

Gratitude

When you know that the visible supply in the Universe is nearly inexhaustible and the invisible supply really is inexhaustible, it's not too difficult to be grateful for what you desire. Not one person is poor because there's not enough to go around. It is usually caused by focusing on lack. So whatever it is that you desire, know that it's available and be in an attitude of gratitude. Even if you're at rock bottom and want to change the direction of your life, be grateful and know that help is on the way. Think health when inundated with the fear of disease. Think abundance when inundated with the appearance of lack. Once you develop the power to change your circumstances, you'll become a master at obtaining whatever your heart desires.

Think health when inundated with the fear of disease. Think abundance when inundated with the appearance of lack.

Tap into a feeling of deep gratitude by simply knowing that the Universe is here for you. Here to protect you, to love you, to grant your wishes so you can become the shining light you were meant to be. God's single point of expression is love, and when you are the shining light, you are the love of God.

There's something about gratitude that keeps the connection switch with the Universe on. It seems to bring us closer to the source. I know it does with me but, then again, I have an incredible life-changing experience to share with the world. Every morning when I get up and put my feet on the floor, I am grateful. There are some mornings when the arthritic effect of my accident rears its ugly head, but I am just as grateful. Gratitude allows you to block out fear and doubt, topics I will discuss soon.

Have you ever noticed in the New Testament that Jesus asks in gratitude when praying to God? He already knew his desires were being created. Gratefulness puts you in a state of mind that your desire is already here, and if you truly believe you have your desire, the Universe's only choice is to bring it into your reality. Gratefulness further allows creative energy to come into being by showing your complete acceptance in advance. In Mark 11:24, it says, "Whatsoever you ask for in prayer, believe that you have received it, and it will be yours."

Remember, thought is your reality. Everything you see around you is a result of the creative ability of thought. Once Universal energy gets to work, it creates in the physical plane. Creating a thought and being in gratitude about the thought produces a physical result. Being grateful about a thought also assists Universal energy in producing the desired result by separating the definitive thought from a wanting of something. This wanting is merely a statement of lack, and that is what would be produced when it's your focus. Eliminate the fear and worry. Be grateful.

Remember, thought is your reality. Everything you see around you is a result of the creative ability of thought.

Forming the Picture

So what additional techniques will help you get what you want? As you clear out old thought patterns, decide what you really want, and develop a clear vision while being in gratitude, there are other steps you can take to help the process along the way.

Basically, these other techniques help you tune in better to your vision of what you want. The clearer you are in your desires, the stronger they become. The stronger they become, the easier it is to hold the thought of what you want. The more you hold onto the thought of what you want, the clearer the desire becomes, and so forth and so on. It can become a deliciously energized circle of thought, focus, and clarity that sends out energy to the Universe, and the Universe responds. The intensity of the energy is more important than to just see the picture clearly. If you just visualize a lazy picture of "Oh, this would be nice someday" without any energetic charge to it, you are nothing more than a dreamer. You have the ability to be so much more! Take that same picture and charge it with the energy of determination to have it. Actually create the feeling of already having it and using it, and see how quickly it comes to you.

Until you become a master at this, here are some steps that will assist you in taking a thought and manifesting it into reality. Personally, I have been blessed with an incredible gift of closing off the outside world and focusing on something I really, really want. If it weren't for this trait, I don't know how I would have been able to deal with my accident and overcoming the paralysis because it was so horrific.

Let me give you a lighter example. When I wrote the page you are reading, I was a partner in a construction company and needed to get in contact with one of my subcontractors because something important had come up. However, when I dialed his number, I found that it had been disconnected. I tried several times throughout the day and got the same result. Not obsessively, mind you, but I kept this thought that I needed to get in contact with him as I went to bed that night, and it was my first thought when I awoke the next morning. When I got to the office, I tried a contact of his who might know his new number. That also proved futile. I mentioned the situation to my business partner but told him it would resolve itself. Remember, I needed to get in contact with him because it was important. Less than an hour later, my phone rang with a strange number on the Caller ID. It was the person I needed to get in contact with! He was calling me to apologize for not letting me know his new cell phone number. These types of things happen to me all the time. Now I expect them; before, they would freak me out!

Here are some tips to help you along your path toward attaining your desires:

Writing: Make a list of the things you most want to create. Write each one out very specifically and in the positive form. Create statements that start out with "I have" or "I am" and not statements like "I want." If you put the energy of wanting out to the Universe, that is what you'll get back. For instance, "I want a BMW." Well, you will continue having a feeling of want for that car, and nothing more. If you have the confidence that you know it will come, it will. It ultimately comes down to knowing versus hoping. Put your heart and soul into it. It's not just some sort of academic exercise. This is your life!

Mental Pictures: Go through the written statements you just created one by one. Take your time and soak them in. Form a specific picture of each one in your mind. Use your five senses with your mental picture. Touch it, smell it, hear it, see it, and taste it. Take this a step further. Combine a few of them and see how they change your life. Details, details, and more details; imagine it as if you were actually experiencing it. Visualization is very important!

In the construction business, I use the visualization process *a lot*. I have to take a set of two-dimensional drawings from an architect and build a structure. With every project—whether it's a home, office building, or shopping center—I study the plans and visualize in my mind what the structure is going to look like. This is no different than when we wish to manifest anything into our life. You think about what you desire, and after much thought, you sketch together an out-

234 / UNINTENDED CONSEQUENCES

line of what you want. You may not be exactly sure as to all the details, but you have a general idea what it is you want. That is your two-dimensional blueprint.

At various points in the construction process, I visit the project to see what progress has been made. More importantly, while I walk through a new home, as an example, I am constantly envisioning what the next few steps are. For instance, after the drywall has been installed and finished, I am envisioning what the interior trim will look like, what the walls will look like when they are painted, and what the flooring is going to look like. *You get the idea.* Although I study what has been done, I don't focus my attention there. Instead it's on what I want next, and through a process similar to this, you will draw toward you what your desires are. You may not know the specific steps necessary, but that doesn't matter. By looking for a moment where you are, you can see the progress you have made. And by continuing the visualization process in as much detail as you can, you make the next steps in the evolution come to fruition.

I used the construction analogy because it's something that is second nature to me. However I've learned to use this same process to work on other things I desire. This book was one of them. Writing a book was something totally foreign to me. I knew nothing about the process involved. Yet, as you can see, you are holding the book in your hands. Stepping into the unknown was somewhat scary, but I believed in my dream and let nothing stop me. As I kept moving forward with a vision of my final goal, people, experiences, and odd coincidences occurred. Take my word for it, *visualization works!* So try it out for yourself.

Visual Aids: I've known people who have developed their own imagination board. They swear by it. Here's how it's done.

You cut out pictures of things you desire and set them up on a board that you can look at. Get a picture of the car you want, the picture of what your perfect mate would look like, and the picture of your new home, and paste or tack them on a board made of any material you may choose. Start out with one board. Once you begin to see results, you may want to develop one board for each area of your life that you're looking to improve: health, money, career, relationships, etc. Place each board in a spot where you can look at it every day. Even glancing at it will refocus your brain to concentrate on achieving your desires. You can use things other than creation boards, though. Someone gave me a $1,000,000 bill (play money, of course) that I carry around with me on my money clip. Every time I pull the clip out of my pocket, it reenergizes my focus on financial abundance.

What If?

"What if" questions are important to be aware of, such as *"What should I do if fear and doubt begin to creep in?"* Perhaps I shouldn't say "if" but "when" because there *will* be a time when fear and doubt inevitably creep in. Remember, as I have discussed, the Universe is neutral and doesn't differentiate between the positive thoughts we focus on and the negative ones. So if you focus on good, positive thought patterns, the Universe will respond in kind. Conversely, if you focus on negative thought patterns, the Universe will respond in a similar way once again.

Most people spend their entire lives living in fear, continuously doubting themselves and worrying about not having what they want. That was the type of household I was raised in. For some reason, I still had an optimistic nature deep within me, and it wasn't until I went away to college that I

236 / UNINTENDED CONSEQUENCES

began to see the world through a different set of eyes—the eyes of opportunity. We all have that chance, no matter how dismal our current situation may seem.

Most people spend their entire lives living in fear, continuously doubting themselves and worrying about not having what they want.

The problem with mental habits, such as fear, worry, and doubt, is that you can begin to have negative thoughts and not even be aware of it. There are tens of thousands of unconscious thoughts that play like a soundtrack in our head every day, and it is these thought patterns that create and shape our reality. Stop sleepwalking through life. Life is not just happening to you. You need to share in the responsibility to be able to change, and you can by improving the quality of your thoughts.

Begin the work by consciously monitoring your thoughts. Consider what you are thinking about. When you realize a negative thought has entered your mind, change the thought to something positive. This takes practice; however, with a little work, it will be an easy game to play. Stay focused on this process.

Once you start to focus on the positive and your desires, you will start to see changes begin to happen. I know I did, but at some point, negative people will show up or doubt will begin to surface. This may be telling someone else what your plans are only to hear "you won't be able to do that." It is at these moments when we need to dig deep within ourselves to resist the inner feeling to give up. I know it was difficult for me at an early age to hear someone tell me I wouldn't be able to accomplish something, but I ultimately used that as motivation to work to achieve it.

Today I use other people's negative comments as a badge of honor, so to speak, to assist me along my way. Now you may not be at that point in your life right now, but you can work to get there. You should certainly not surround yourself with negative people because it will hold you back and make it difficult to gain a positive outlook. Surround yourself with positive people, and then on the occasions when you find yourself in the company of negative people, try not to share your goals and dreams with them. Recognize that if you do, they will thrive on killing the dreams. Realize that you don't have to fall into their thought pattern. Smile and walk away with your positive attitude in place. I often bless them and ask that they receive what they truly want rather than all that they fear.

Note that if you focus your attention on your current circumstances, that is what your experience is going to continue to be. If that is what you really want, then keep doing it. If you don't, then start to focus on things you do want. If you continue to focus on how things always turned out in the past, that is what you will continue to perpetuate. The real answer is that we can affect the outcome of our situation by using our thought process. If you are a people pleaser, *You can ask for the* like I used to be, then you will help others get *best possible out-* what they want at your own expense. Learn *come for everyone* to be okay with yourself and focus more on *who will be affected.* your desires. Focus on your desires, but not at the expense of others. You can ask for the best possible outcome for everyone who will be affected. That is not putting anyone in front of your dreams; it gives you the freedom to know that you have no control over how others will feel about your success. Know that while the ripple affects others, it is their choice in how they allow your success to move their life. Remember, we want to create rather than compete.

It's difficult to master the mental game, but when accomplished, it is one of the keys to life. Changing the thought process is more difficult than changing a physical habit. I know it can be done because I have worked with some very negative-thinking people to change their thought habits. Granted, they may not have become totally positive people, but they do think differently than before, and positively more often.

Time for Action

Okay, let's say that you have formulated a clear picture of your desire and have also followed every step previously outlined. Now you must take on the task of doing whatever is required of you as the Universe works with you. If not, you will be nothing more than a dreamer and only have unfulfilled requests. You must work with the Universe to bring about your desires. As things unfold, and they will, you must

You must work with the Universe to bring about your desires. be ready to make decisions about the direction your life will take. Maintain the faith that whatever your desire is, it's already yours. Focus on it mentally with your thoughts. Act as if it is already here. Continue your gratitude. No matter what may appear to be happening around you, maintain your vision. The Universe wants to give you what you want.

When a plane takes off from New York for Los Angeles, a detailed flight plan has been established. What route to take, how much fuel will be required, how high and how fast to travel, and so on—the smallest detail has been taken into account. However, because of gravitational forces, the plane must start making adjustments shortly after takeoff. The pilots must keep their focus on the original flight plan and make adjustments as they go. That is what you must do to be successful in creating the life you want.

Once you put your intention out to the Universe, you must be diligent in looking and listening for signs. People, circumstances, and situations will begin to occur that will assist you in getting what you want. You may have thought out your desire to the smallest detail, but sometimes the Universe has other methods and manners for your desire to unfold. *Listen. Watch. Be ready.* You will be meeting people or experiencing events that you could never have envisioned, and these experiences will point you in the direction of your desire. *Be available for anything.*

There is no master plan. There are many ways to approach this method of creating what you want. Even before I knew about this process, I was able to create things in my life. The old me always was the one who would try to force things to happen. Needless to say, even though there were times when I got what I wanted, there were just as many times when it didn't happen, or at least didn't happen the way I wanted. Once I learned this process, things flowed much more easily to me, but you still need vision plus action. Even if you're currently in a situation (job, relation- *Find the blessing in what you have.* ship) that you don't necessarily want, rather than continuing to focus on those things you're unhappy with, focus on what you want while doing your best in whatever your current situation is. Find the blessing in what you have. What was it you liked about that situation that you want to continue into the new one? Be grateful for those things in the old one that you want in the new one. Letting go of the old while in gratitude allows the Universe to open up and direct you to your true desires.

As I look back on my own life, I see a series of situations and opportunities that have occurred which have caused me to investigate the "why." And especially after my accident, my soul has yearned for meaning: *the meaning of life and why we are here, the purpose we all have, and what we can accomplish.*

Many people have an opportunity to have one teacher who shows them the process. I haven't had one guru who has appeared from the "mist" to enlighten me. Instead, life experience has been my science experiment, with many people popping in and out as co-scientists, both as teachers and students, often without either of us knowing what was occurring. This is a simple method of how we can create, and I have learned it by living it. If you never actually believed such a process was possible, keep an open mind and give it a try. What can it hurt? See if it works as well for you as it does for me. Let life become your petri dish. You'll be amazed by the results.

Chapter 14

The Spiritual Side of Success

WE HAVE DISCUSSED AT GREAT LENGTH HOW we create our reality, whether we like what we have or not. Rather than drift along in life's currents, we have a say in which direction we head. As we begin to make these conscious decisions, we need to be able to define what our idea of success is and how it makes us feel. Being able to define success, and how it affects our lives, enables us to be truly authentic people.

I can certainly attest, at least in my personal experience, that success is not just a compilation of material possessions. At age 26, I started my first business. Within six months, my partner and I purchased a matching set of Porsche 911s. As I look back on that time, I can honestly say that I was just as miserable after I bought that car as I was before I had it. And the same level of misery remained even after I sold it 16 months later. It wasn't the car that made me miserable. The car was just a car; the misery was that I wasn't satisfied with who I was or with the accomplishments I had achieved. The car that I thought would make me happy was just not enough, and that made it frustrating. I expected to really be happy with this purchase, which would show the world I had arrived.

The problem is that material things are not what delights our spirit. I was miserable before, and without finding what I truly wanted, I was miserable afterward. It isn't a bad thing to want material objects like a Porsche; just don't expect them to fix any problems you may have, unless transportation is your problem and you don't need trunk space!

I've spoken to countless people through the years to see if material possessions were the cause of their happiness and contentment. I needed some reassurance that I wasn't alone in not finding satisfaction there because I know it never worked for me. And 99 percent of the time, I got the reassurance I was seeking. We all have this inner black hole that we try to fill with outside trinkets, thinking they're going to make us feel better. Sometimes they do, but usually not for long!

> We all have this inner black hole that we try to fill with outside trinkets, thinking they're going to make us feel better. Sometimes they do, but usually not for long!

I have had a beautiful home in a prestigious neighborhood. It didn't do it. I've had a boat I kept in a marina on the Chesapeake Bay. Nice, very nice, but alas, it didn't do it either! I continually strived to find the next possession to make myself feel good but never quite found it. In fact, it wasn't until I moved to Florida ten years ago and lost everything that I was forced to look within to see where my discontent originated. This is what I came up with.

The biggest lesson I've learned is becoming okay with myself. People continually ask me, "Exactly what do you mean by that statement?" My easiest definition would be that *I do not need to look for some outside source (person or thing) to make me feel worthy.* It has been a long, slow inner evolution/revolution for me. However, I now know that I'm okay just the way I currently am. I don't need to prove anything to anyone. I don't need to own anything to prove my worth. I have spent so many years just trying to do that, and I fully understand now that I don't need to prove anything.

Success & Fulfillment

I have discovered what my true primary values are. I work at being my authentic self. By learning to be true to myself, I realized that I didn't need to please others in order to gain approval, and that's not being selfish. My happiness, peace, and contentment come from the inside and not from something outside. I have also found that the less I force life, the more it flows for me.

We only need to look inward to see potential, or possibilities, within. On my journey, I eventually got to know the inner me, but only after I allowed it to happen. I ran away from myself for so many years! Finally I realized that everything I needed to become a "success" was already in my possession. I suppose I should say "fulfilled" rather than a success. I know when I am fulfilled but cannot always tell you when I am a success.

Success grows when you feel good about yourself. Being a success on the inside will reflect upon your outside world.

For the sake of this conversation, I will continue to use the word "success" because I realize I am, in fact, a success at every moment. I know the more I connect with my inner spirit, and co-creator, the more I can create of whatever my desire measures as success. I also know I don't have to become a monk or sell all the worldly possessions that I may have. You can be in harmony with your spiritual essence while achieving outward materialistic success. However, if you think you're going to be a success only after that BMW shows up in your driveway, *think again.*

Success grows when you feel good about yourself. Being a success on the inside will reflect upon your outside world.

Happiness is a choice. It's a continuous choice. Happy and content people are the ones who are successful. Know who you are and what you are capable of in this world. Realize your connection with the Universe. This will allow you to move past your fears and inner demons and on to the life you have always dreamed about. Follow your heart and don't be afraid to pursue your dreams. Many times, we are afraid and end up living a life of unfulfilled potential.

Worldly success can be arbitrary. To me, it may mean one thing, but to you, it could be something entirely different. For many years, success was some sort of destination for me. "I'll be a success only after …" or "I'll be a success when I achieve. …" On July 11, 1989, I realized that if I continued to think along those lines, I might never be able to consider myself a success. I know success is for me to be the best I can be today and every day. It is to leave the ego part out of it and enjoy what's happening at this moment. It's all about the journey and not what the destination might be. If you can find peace and contentment within your soul, you're on the way to success. Connecting with your inner source will allow you to define your true purpose rather than run from it. Combining purpose with an inner connection will certainly allow you to live a successful life.

Understand that it is all right to be in the unknown. We always want our path illuminated, but true growth and success is being able to be in the unknown.

Another major key is to learn to live a balanced life between the spiritual world and material world. You may have all the possessions in the world; however, if you live in a state of constant fear and anxiety, what good is it?

Ladies and gentlemen, this is not rocket science. Learn to quiet your mind, go beyond the ego, and listen to the still small voice within. It will never lead you astray. Understand that it is all right to be in the unknown. We always want our path illuminated, but true growth and success is being able to be in the unknown. The Universe will not let you down. It will show you what the next step is on the way to becoming your true authentic self, and that's the greatest level of success one can achieve. Dr. Martin Luther King said, "Faith is taking the first step, even when you don't see the whole staircase." Take that first step and everything else will fall into place.

If you think you cannot be both spiritually and materialistically successful in harmony, ponder this: "Seek ye first the kingdom of God, and all other things shall be added unto you." (Matthew 6:33) It took me many, many years to understand this passage. Many of those years I fought it tooth and nail. But once I realized that in God's eyes I am perfect as I am right now, life began to fall into place. And when you have the opportunity in life to have an "aha" moment like that, life itself can be quite exhilarating!

Chapter 15

It's All in Your Head—So Make Life Work for You!

YOU ARE THE SUM TOTAL OF YOUR THOUGHTS. As within, so without. However you want to phrase it, the one common denominator is that our reality is affected by our thoughts. It is shaped by the predominant thoughts that become the movie in our head. How we feel, what we think of ourselves, and how we judge something all affect our perception of reality. The key is to be conscious of our thoughts so we can exert control over them, or "weed the garden" so to speak.

Every one of us has incredible inner power at our disposal 24 hours a day, seven days a week. The successful among us are the ones who, knowingly or unknowingly, tap into this source.

In the past few years, the movie and book *The Secret* exploded onto the scene with the theory that we merely need to think about what we want and it will appear. This is a kind of Consciousness 101 combined with the Law of Attraction. It definitely presents beneficial principles, but if you're not okay with yourself as yourself, what good is that BMW sitting in your driveway?

This "mind stuff" has been around forever. Wallace D. Wattles wrote a book in 1908 titled *The Science of Getting*

Rich. It's available on the Internet as a free download. I think it's fascinating. Another example, and this one has become my bible, is *The Master Key System* by Charles F. Haanel. This was originally published in 1912. It started out as a 24-part study course Haanel mailed to people who paid $1,500—an unheard of price at that time. Only the wealthy could afford it. Once Haanel decided to publish the entire *Master Key System* as a book, it sold more than 200,000 copies before it was banned by the church and virtually disappeared by 1933.

During the 1980s, it was widely reported that many of the entrepreneurs in Silicon Valley had come across this book and become believers in its contents. Many stories have circulated that Bill Gates got his hands on a copy of it while at Harvard. With his commitment to purpose and the contents of the book at his disposal, it is reported that Gates dropped out of Harvard and began his quest to put a computer on every desk.

Everything we are at this point today is a direct result of how we think about ourselves.

In the book, Haanel notes, "We must 'be' before we can 'do,' and we can 'do' only to the extent which we 'are,' and what we 'are' depends upon what we 'think.'" Everything we are at this point today is a direct result of how we think about ourselves. There is a world within each of us which is reflected by a world without. The world without is strictly a reflection of the world within. That is where our power comes from. We have the ability to influence the world within strictly by how we think. The world within is governed by mind. Once we grasp this concept and understand it, every answer to every problem will surface. It is all within our control.

Visualizing

Mental imaging (visualization) has been huge in the sports arena over the past few decades. Sports psychologists working with athletes have shown measurable results in this field. These professionals hooked up the track stars to machines to measure electrical impulses in their bodies. The tests have shown that when a track participant focuses mentally on running a race, electric impulses from muscle groups occur as if the athlete is actually running the race—not just focusing on it in the mind.

Different uses of imagery in sports include the mental practice of specific performance skills, improving confidence and positive thinking, problem-solving, controlling anxiety, performance analysis, and preparation for performance. All these things are used in the ability to create our reality. It's all what we think about, what we focus on, and what we think about ourselves that brings it about.

Mental imaging works because when we imagine ourselves performing a task to perfection and doing exactly what we want, we are creating neural patterns in the brain (physiologically speaking)—just as if we had physically performed the task. These create patterns in the brain that can enable us to perform physical feats simply by mentally practicing the task. The mental imagery is intended to train the mind and create neural patterns in the brain to teach the muscles to do exactly what we want them to do.

The US Olympic Committee, Performance Services Division, has a publication called the *Sports Psychology Mental Training Manual*. Chapters in the manual include goal-setting, mental imagery, self-talk, concentration, self-confidence, and mental preparation, to name but a few. They also sell accompanying videos for the athletes to study. It has been proven in the sports world that mental imagery works. So why not learn to use it for your own life?

Taking Responsibility

Most people today are so conditioned by their past that they live in a constant state of stagnation or, even worse, in a destructive state, not even knowing the awesome potential they have within themselves readily at their disposal. They live their lives every day not knowing this inner potential and continue on a daily basis just to exist. They accept their lives and what they have because they don't know any better.

I see it in people every day in every walk of life. Many complain, but very few are willing to do whatever it takes to change. Their current state may be painful, but it is familiar. They know the pain, but another course of action is too unknown. Yet we all can control our destiny. We all have the ability to change and stop perpetuating our misery. It took me many years to understand that. Because I have had the opportunity to be shown and to understand, I know I am now continuing to move forward and seek my truth.

Many complain, but very few are willing to do whatever it takes to change. Their current state may be painful, but it is familiar.

I am a very big believer in *personal responsibility*. Everything I shared about myself in the earlier sections of this book is strictly to lay a foundation, and that foundation is basically that it doesn't matter what has happened to you in life but, rather, what you do about it. I don't seek sympathy for my accident and what I had to do to heal.

Our lives develop through natural laws and by the choices we make. I take responsibility for everything that has happened to me in my life. I don't feel that life has been unfair or that I deserve anything special because of my accident. I don't need any mulligans (a replay of a shot in golf) or do-overs. On the contrary, I wouldn't change anything that has happened during the course of my life. It has made me the person I am now.

Granted, a different choice here or there along the way may have changed the path I took. However, I accept everything the way it has happened because, based on the choices I have made, I have steered the raft of my life to the location where it is today. Where will it be tomorrow? I have absolutely no idea, but I do know this—based on what I've learned, I know that my choices carry great weight, and I intend to make the best choices possible for me based on the laws of the Universe. And I will choose to apply them in the most positive way I know how.

In my situation, the biggest life lesson so far has been learning to become okay with me. I am good just the way I am. It, unfortunately, took a near-death experience for life to allow me to revisit my perception of reality and therefore my perception of truth. Prior to the accident, I had listened to and bought into too much negativity. I allowed it to creep in and control me through the ego. It had become my existence.

My dysfunctional childhood kept me in a survival mode where it seemed there was no hope, only a matter of hanging on. Yet, even in that childhood home environment, seeds were inside of me that maintained an uncertain level of hope that things could and would get better someday. My ship would come in. I began to see that life was not black and white but, rather, various shades of gray. To me, gray means infinite possibilities of choices—not just either/or. It is how you use those choices that determines the direction your life heads.

My problem, which I was not conscious of at that time, was that I had become an angry young man. Immense inner anger was seething within me because I felt life had treated me unfairly. I was not going to allow it to happen to me again. I built up such incredibly high walls around my personal "space" that I never let anyone in, including myself. I could never let anyone see who I really was. I took vulnerability as a sign of weakness. This stemmed from self-blame for my negative childhood experiences. How could I have let that happen to me? I was on my own now; nobody and nothing was going to put me in a situation I didn't want to be in. I didn't want anyone to see the way I perceived myself, just like Frank Morgan's character, the Wizard, in *The Wizard of Oz*. I spent my early adulthood behind a personal "curtain," trying to control every minute aspect of my life. Let me tell you, it was pretty tiresome work. No one could ever harm me, and if I didn't like someone or something, I would just cut ties. I'd "take my beach ball" and go home. This was all strictly based on how my ego thought about things.

In the classic *Oz* movie, the Wizard was perceived to be a very powerful man—as long as no one saw him behind the curtain. Once Toto exposed him, Dorothy and the others saw him to be no different than anybody else. What everyone failed to realize was that he was just as powerful standing in front of the curtain. He provided answers to all, knowing that the answers each were seeking would come from within.

The events surrounding that fateful day in July 1989 actually were the beginning of my curtain being removed. Although it may not seem like it, life gave me an opportunity to show myself what I was made of. I experienced incredible power from within. Power that I knew existed all the time, but power I felt I was not worthy to experience.

I know the night in the hospital when God spoke to me was a moment of true connection with the Universe. That moment was an experience of true unconditional love, probably the first time I had ever experienced something like that. I began to believe that I was worthy, that I meant something.

And no matter the incredible odds, as long as I kept the faith and stayed focused, synchronistic events continued to happen. Ultimately, I walked out of the rehabilitation center.

Seizing Opportunities

Yes, I have been able to overcome some incredible odds, but I am by no means any different than you. We are all equally brilliant, part of the one Universe. It doesn't matter what has happened to you up to this exact moment. You have the ability within to change if you really, truly want to do so. Whether you're facing a dire situation or merely feel a desire to change, you have the power to make your life what you want it to be.

Some things to remember:

1. **We are all created in the image and likeness of God (Genesis 1:26).** This means we are all like God in form, and it implies that we have a spiritual capacity to create.
2. **The seeds of greatness are implanted in each and every one of us,** and they're just waiting for us to grow and blossom. All we need to do is to believe and allow.

Once we realize the immense inner power we have, there are three steps to create what we desire. They really are simple, but we tend to make them difficult. See the list of the three steps.

It sounds simple enough, yet it can be profoundly difficult. Your thoughts got you to where you are today. If you don't like where you are, use your thoughts to change the direction of your life.

Three Steps to Manifesting a Desire

1. We must earnestly desire it.
2. We must assert our claim for it.
3. We must take possession.

Earlier I discussed how we create our reality. But how do we change if we don't like what we're receiving? The steps are pretty basic, but attention to detail provides extraordinary results.

- **Understand that there is but one Universal energy force** from which we all came. All physical life functions in accordance with Universal Laws.

- **Get rid of old negative thought patterns.** This is where we all need to realize that much of what we think has been influenced by others. We need to clean all negative thoughts out and know the truth. Develop new thought patterns based on what you've read here, and see what happens.

- **Discover what you really want.** This will get you started. Define it down to its most minute pieces. See it fully down to every detail. Meditate on what it is that you truly want. You may be surprised at the answer because you have been so busy listening to the ramblings in your current unconscious state.

- **Have a clear vision.** Doing the steps above will assist with this step. A clear vision will help when others try to dissuade you because it is too difficult—*according to them.*

- **Be grateful for your desires.** Be grateful for everything you already have. Also, know that the Universe has an inexhaustible supply to satisfy your every need.

- **Form the picture.** Write out your desires. Keep them where you can continue to refine and review them. Form mental pictures of what it is you want. Hold them firm in your mind. Don't be concerned with how you will achieve it. That part is up to the Universe. Your part is to hold fast to the picture. Use whatever visual aids help, such as drawings, maps, or visualization boards. *Focus, focus, focus.*

- **Be ready for the "what ifs."** *They will come.* Fear and doubt will try to creep in. Old thought patterns will appear. Don't let them take hold. Remember, the Universe doesn't differentiate between positive and negative requests.
- **Then it's time for action.** Once the picture is formed, the Universe will begin its job. Be ready to act when people, situations, and circumstances begin to appear to take you in the direction of your desire. It is a co-creative venture!

You are a success just the way you are today. This goes back to being okay with yourself; you don't need to prove anything to anyone or to own something special to prove your worth.

You have the world at your fingertips. You really do. But there are no two identical paths to God. If there were, someone would have patented them by now and made a tremendous amount of money. The things I have shared in this book have worked for me. Some, I am sure, can assist you.

Continue to strive to live an authentic life and live it now. Find people, books, films, DVDs, or whatever works for you to assist you along your journey. Too often we would rather allow the ego to take control. Then we buy into the get-rich-quick schemes that are presented to us because we think we'll be happy once there's more money. Or we may buy into the latest diet plan blitzed across the TV screen; that way, we can be happy once we get to look like others who are thinner. Or hair replacement … or whatever is being sold to make us feel better about ourselves because we don't think we're good enough now.

True change happens from within, and it starts with how you think about things—most importantly, how you think about yourself.

True change happens from within, and it starts with how you think about things—most importantly, how you think about yourself. I trust something in this book resonated with your core. Earlier in my life, I never had any intention to write a book. It was the furthest thing from my mind. But then I experienced a blessing with my accident that many other people never get the opportunity to receive.

God just wanted me to take a moment and share my experience and lessons learned with you. That is all. Thank you for reading this book. Go out and be the success you were destined to be! God bless you. I know he blesses me, and he blesses us all.

About the Author

Bill Shaner has used the unique blessings learned through tragedy to inspire and encourage countless others to achieve their dreams. He has evolved his life into one of sharing his life lessons with others through speaking and coaching. Bill currently resides in Naples, Florida. Visit Bill Shaner at **www. billshaner.com.**